Widowed
with
Kids

You do it for the kids until you rediscover yourself

Sharon Rosenbloom

Books Boost Business

Books Boost Business is part of Forever Family Forever Free group of Companies whose address can be found at BooksBoostBusiness.com.

This book was created using the "'Idea to Author" done for you service at Books Boost Business.

First published in the United Kingdom.
Edited by Susan Gault & Wendy Helen
Copyright © 2020 by Sharon Rosenbloom

First published 2020: Books Boost Business

Book: Widowed with Kids –

Sharon Rosenbloom

ISBN-13: 978-1-913501-10-5

Foreword

*Since connecting with Sharon, she has truly transformed
from someone full of fear with no self-belief. Sharon had
become stuck in a cycle since losing her husband. It took
her 18 years and some great connections to shake off those
old patterns and really find herself. Sharon has helped
many widows and widowers through their grief journey
whilst at the same time supporting their children.
Sharon's book is a great example of her strength and
character, a true diamond in the world of grief and
bereavement. It is a story of truths and courage from
beginning to end and demonstrates her love for her
husband and her children. It is going to make you laugh
and cry. It is a true reflection of a mother's journey through
grief whilst supporting her children to the best of her
ability. This book will pull on your heartstrings whilst giving
you hope and faith that, no matter what life throws at you,
there is always a way out, a way back to the true you.
There is always a future even if we don't see it. Sharon's*

ability to help people in their darkest times to see the light is truly incredible.

She is a great friend, a true inspiration of courage, and I admire her as an incredibly strong parent.

Thank you, Sharon, for sharing your toughest times with us.

Laura Helen

International Speaker, Parent Coach & Number One
Bestselling Author

Preface

Thank you for taking the time to read this book, as there are numerous reasons why I have written it. First, it's my tribute to my wonderful husband Simon Paul Rosenbloom (1960-2002).

Simon would have been 60 this year 2020. I believe this is a perfect year to launch this book.

Secondly, I am passionate in supporting you in your time of need. I know Simon would be honoured and so very proud of me for doing this to support you, and to help you through your darkest times to eventually see the light at the end of a very dark tunnel.

It has taken me seventeen years to really move forward with my life. You will never completely get over losing your husband, wife, partner or loved one. But you can learn to live without putting a mask on every day, and my passion is to help you to see this.

I lost myself in my grief and felt like I was the victim for far too long.

This is also for my two beautiful children, Sophie and Oliver, who I love so very much, and who are the reason that I am still here to write this book.

If you are grieving while reading this, my hope is that it gives you some extra support.

If you are not grieving, please pass it on after you have read it to somebody in need. Don't let them struggle alone.

Much love to you all.

Sharon xxx

Author and Grief Specialist Coach

Endorsements

Working with Sharon over the last couple of years has shown me a remarkable example of growth and determination. I've seen her go from being someone who apologised every few words (no exaggeration here) to someone who has become a beacon of light for our women's network. Sharon is committed to growth and learning in an impressive way that impacts her life and that of her whole family. She is an example of integrity and joy to us all.

Anna Garcia

What I love most about Sharon is her appetite for life, growth and development. It's so important to her that you can't help but want to be part of it. It's been a real privilege and beauty to see my friend grow. To see how she's overcome challenges and how she's still had a wonderful sense of humour through it all. I'm beyond proud of you Sharon in writing this book and sharing your journey with others with the intention of being a light, so people know they are not alone and can overcome anything.

With love, Gozi.

I first met Sharon a year ago, very sweet, kind and generous. Still all these things and more, but I first saw the real Sharon during a photoshoot in my studio in London. She is bold, beautiful and courageous, she has found her sparkle in her eyes and owns her voice. Congratulations Sharon, you are an inspiration.

Rodney Pedroza Portraits
Photographer and friend

It's amazing to see how far you have come over the years I've known you, all the fears you have overcome head on and your 'go get 'em' attitude. This book has spoken to you so you can speak to others. Every success as you continue to move forward in life.

Paula x

Table of Contents

The Most Traumatic Day of My Life

15th June 2002 was the most traumatic day of my life. It was the day that Simon, my husband, my soulmate and my best friend, finally lost his life after an awful battle with cancer.

Simon was only forty-one when he died, I was thirty-nine. We had two young children who were seven and five. That day was the worst day of my life, and the day that the dynamics of my family changed completely.

Simon was in a hospice in the final stages of his life. I received a call saying that I needed to get there quickly. Sophie was at school and Oliver was at home with me so I had to wait for my friend to come round to look after Oliver while her husband took me to the hospice. By the time we got there, Simon had passed away.

I was absolutely terrified as I had never seen a dead body before and I couldn't even go into his room when I first got there, as I was too scared. The lovely nurse who was on duty said she would come with me, but my body just froze and I couldn't move.

My friend had phoned Sophie's school and Simon's friend Farrell brought Sophie to the hospice. Once Sophie arrived at the hospice, we went into Simon's room together and she climbed on the bed and lay with him. That was so hard for me to see. A young child lying on the bed with her dead father. I was trying to stay strong in front of Sophie but I just broke down and was crying uncontrollably.

This was the day that my life was totally shattered. I felt so crushed, scared and alone. I felt totally numb and shocked. Why has this happened to me? Yesterday, I was married to a wonderful man and now I'm widowed with two young kids. Inside my head, I screamed, 'Life shouldn't happen like this when I'm only thirty-nine.' I felt that I must have been a very bad person in my past life for this to happen to me.

I felt totally overwhelmed and didn't want to be here anymore. I felt so empty without him, and I had a huge hole in my heart. I felt physically sick all the time and I just couldn't stop crying.

I wasn't functioning properly and felt like I was in thick dark fog. Grief is the longest road you will ever travel along. It's very dark, foggy and absolutely terrifying, and it seems like it will never end. Some roads are slow and dark, with lots of bumps and hold-ups. Grieving is the longest, slowest process you have to go through. It's as if you are on a long frightening journey.

Everyone is unique and nobody grieves in the same way. Take as long as you need to reach the fast roads, or stay on the slow roads and they will eventually not be so dark and frightening.

In the early days, I was so overwhelmed with grief, I was totally lost. How was I going to bring up my two children on my own?

I felt so sad that Simon would not see them growing up. He would not be there to see them reaching all their milestones. How was I going to run the household on my own? Simon dealt with all the financial affairs, and I looked after the household and the kids, with an immense amount of support from him. Oliver has complex special needs and is very challenging. He has Autism, Dyspraxia, ADHD, learning disabilities, speech impairments and global delay.

Bedtime was the worst time for me as that is when I felt most alone. When I closed my bedroom door and got into bed, that is when I felt the pain the most. I was totally lost and alone, and had no one to talk to, to say how my day had been, no one to have a hug with or any intimacy. I felt my heart was in bits. I just did not want to be here anymore.

Simon was diabetic and I had a lot of insulin in the fridge. So many times I wanted to give myself a massive dose. Thank goodness I was afraid of needles. Thank goodness for our children. They were the only reason I got out of bed in the mornings, as I had to get them ready for school.

I was a comfort eater and I ate my way through my emotions and feelings, rather than feel them. Subsequently I put on nearly five stone, which I will talk about more in another chapter.

During a bereavement, many people eat more, or they just cannot eat at all. Some people turn to drink, or drugs, or smoking, or shopping, or some other addiction.

Grief never ends, but over time, it changes.

Saying Goodbye, The Funeral

We are a Jewish family, and in the Jewish religion, the funeral is usually carried out within a day or two of the person passing away unless there are complications with the death.

I was fortunate that my brother and brother-in-law organised all the funeral arrangements and registration of the death.

In the Jewish religion, women should not attend a funeral if their parents are still alive, and both my parents were still alive. Also children are not meant to attend a funeral if they are under the age of thirteen.

Officially, both Sophie and I shouldn't have been at my husband's funeral. Obviously, that did not happen.

I do believe the older generation did not think that Sophie should have been there. I did not want her to think when she was older that I did not allow her to attend her father's funeral. So, I sat down with her and gave her the choice. I spoke to her about the funeral and then told her it was her choice. I said she could go and stay with one of her friends, if she wanted, or she could come with me to the funeral. Sophie chose to come with me. It was different with Oliver. He stayed at home with a friend of mine.

5

It was very unfortunate that the date of Simon's funeral was also Father's Day. Sophie had made a lovely card for Simon at school. In the Jewish religion, you are buried undressed and wrapped in a shroud. Nothing is allowed in the coffin with the physical body, but Sophie really wanted to put the card inside with him. We had a lovely Reverend taking the service and he let her put the card inside.

The service was held in a very dark cold room, with the women on one side and the men on the other side. The Rabbi stood at the front, in the middle of the men and women.

I felt totally numb. There were hundreds of people there and I just felt like an alien it was so surreal. The prayer hall was very cold and quiet, and you could hear a pin drop. I felt as though someone had ripped out my heart and I was screaming inside.

I have always felt guilty about what I wore on the day. I wore a summery skirt and a white shirt. Thinking about that now, it really does not matter what other people thought about me. I had just lost my husband, my best friend and my soulmate. I absolutely hated the world right then and thought why has this happened to me and my two beautiful children.

There was a short service before the actual burial and then people were invited back to my house where the main mourners sat on low uncomfortable chairs for five days of mourning. This is called 'sitting Shiva'.

Sitting Shiva, In Mourning

Sitting Shiva comes from the word shiva, which means seven, signifying the seven days of mourning. It's a time for spiritual and emotional healing, where mourners join together.

The Shiva is usually held at the family's home. It's traditionally held for a seven-day period, or one day for those who are not so religious.

Mirrors, televisions and computer screens are also covered as a way to remind us that, during the seven-day period, it is not about ourselves, but a time to concentrate on the deceased. This is a time of self-reflection, to concentrate on one's inner self and not outward appearances.

There were three of us sitting Shiva – myself, my mother-in-law Estelle and my brother-in-law Barry. If you are under thirteen years old, you don't sit Shiva.

People come to your home for prayers at 8pm and a short service is given by the Rabbi. Family and friends stay to give you comfort and support for an hour or two afterwards. Some people also come round in the afternoon so you are not alone.

I am not religious but we sat Shiva for the week. I am pleased I did, as it is a great support, because you are not on your own. But after the last person left at around 9pm or 10pm, and I had closed the door, sorted out the children and put them to bed, I felt totally lost and alone. Then I would simply just break down and cry.

Bedtime was the worst time for me. It was the time that I felt truly alone and lost. I hardly slept at all. I was lucky if I got sixty minutes sleep a night. I used to just cry myself to sleep, but no sooner had I fallen asleep than I would once again be awake.

Many people used to tell me to take sleeping tablets, but I did not want to as I was afraid of becoming addicted to them, plus I was on anti-depressants at the time.

After a few weeks, I gave in and started taking Nytol, which I could buy over the counter. In the beginning, I took the recommended amount and it did help me to sleep a little bit better.

When morning finally came, I just did not want to get out of bed, but I had to get Sophie and Oliver ready for school. If I had not had children to look after, I would probably have just stayed in bed all day, as I did not want to face the world alone.

The Stone Setting

The stone setting is the very ancient Jewish tradition of placing a monument over the grave of a departed person. It marks the final resting place and honours the person's life.

It is usually held within the first year. Ours was eight months after Simon died. About a week before the stone setting, I went to the cemetery when I was told that the headstone had been put up. I just broke down when I saw it. I could not believe that was where Simon was laying, so alone.

I now recommend to other people to do the same, to visit the headstone before the service, rather than to wait for the day of the actual service, as I personally believe it is much harder seeing it for the first time with all your friends and family with you. Looking back, maybe it would have been better if I'd gone with one close friend.

On the day of the service, I brought a small notebook and put a post-it note on the front which said:
'Please write whatever you are thinking or feeling or what you would have liked to have said to Simon.'

9

I wrote the very first memory:

I am sure no one wants to be the first person to write in this book, so I will start:

Simon, you know how much I love and miss you, and I hope things are better for you now, and you are enjoying Pamela's mum's roast potatoes.
I cannot say my final goodbyes to you as I feel that part of you will always be with me.
As Sophie would say
"love you to infinity"
And as Oliver would say,
"Uv Ou"
xxx

I came crashing down after the stone setting. Many people seem to think that you should feel better after the stone setting. Although if they have not lost their husband, their best friend, their soul mate, their life, how would they understand the tangled web of feelings that I was going through.

Life with Simon

Simon was an exceptionally good man. He was honest, kind, compassionate and had a great sense of humour. He needed to have, living with me. He worked very hard. He was a pharmacist, employed by Boots the Chemist, and also a Store Manager. He did not smoke or drink, and he gave money every month to a charity.

Simon first became ill when he was twenty-eight. He had cancer of the pancreas. It took a long time for the doctors to actually find it. At first, they thought he was an alcoholic, as one day they asked him what he'd drunk the previous night and he did have a lager, which he really didn't like. Simon's drink was diet coke! I do believe that the symptoms that an alcoholic suffers from are similar to symptoms of cancer of the pancreas.

After a lot of surgery, Simon was in a private hospital, so in his own room, and he had a heart attack. Thank God his friend Julian was there visiting him at the time.

People with pancreatic cancer do not usually have a good survival rate, only 7% survive more than five years. Less than 2% are alive after ten years.

Widowedwithkids.co.uk

Fortunately for Simon and me, I did not know him when he first had it. He managed nearly fourteen years in remission. Simon did not know that his cancer was malignant when he had it originally. In those times, the doctors did not always tell the patients much detail. My mother-in-law knew. She told me this while I was writing this book. At first, I was annoyed that she had not told him, and then I thought maybe it was a good thing.

I met Simon on a blind date when I was 29 and he was 31. A good friend of mine was going out with one of Simon's closest friends. There is actually a letter from him in the chapter called 'How Simon's Dear Friends Remember Him'.

I actually didn't really want to go, my period had just started and I felt a bit yuk. We went on the M25 motorway and got stuck in traffic for about an hour. I didn't tell my friend but I was thinking 'phew'. We had a nice evening though. And then I spilt a large glass of diet coke all over Simon. It was very difficult not to laugh, and I thought 'he won't phone me'.

But Simon did, he phoned me the following day. When I answered the phone, he said 'hello, it's Simon', and I said 'Simon who?'. He said 'Simon from last night' and I couldn't remember what I'd done the previous night, lol.

We went out again and had a lovely evening. Simon lived in Leatherhead in Surrey and I lived in Stanmore in Middlesex. It used to take Simon an hour and a half each way to get to me, and often longer if he got stuck in traffic. He did this every day for about eight months until I finally moved in with him.

We got married in September 1993. We had a great marriage, the only thing we ever argued over was food. That was because Simon was diabetic, and I was always checking the sugar levels of food. Simon would just eat whatever he wanted.

In September 1994, Sophie was born. That was one of the best days of my life. I so wanted a little girl. I had a perfect birth with her too. I had an epidural and did not feel any labour pains at all. I was watching TV and her head was coming out, but I wanted to wait until I had finished watching Brookside. Sorry Sophie!

Oliver was born in January 1997. Just like each person's grief experience is so different, so is everyone's birth experience. I had an epidural with Oliver as I wanted the same experience as I had had with Sophie, but it was awful. The epidural only worked down one side, the labour pains, which went on for 36 hours, were so intense. Eventually he had to be delivered by forceps.
Whether this caused his disability, I will never know. I had so much anaesthetic being pumped into my body for so long. I do feel now that this may have possibly caused Oliver's disability. Having a forceps delivery must have been so traumatising for a tiny baby. I am not a doctor, so I will never

13

know for sure, but this is my gut instinct. I love Oliver for who he is and would not want him any other way.

Simon and I had a good life together and I felt we had a perfect family.

In September 2001, Simon started to feel unwell. He continued working until it got to the stage where he was feeling so bad that Boots signed him off sick with stress.

At the time, I did not know how badly stress can affect the body. I do not wish to frighten you, but stress can disturb every system and cell in your body. It weakens your immune system, it can upset your digestive system, and it increases your risk of heart attacks and strokes. Stress can also cause pain and soreness in your muscles and joints, as well as emotional symptoms, for example, depression, anxiety, anger, and a sense of loneliness and isolation.

Simon had been so fortunate to be in remission for fourteen years. In September 2001, he started complaining of stomach pains and went to see his oncologist, who gave Simon his usual blood test, which came back as clear. He had many tests and they were all negative.

When his pains started getting more severe, he had a biopsy on his liver.

On New Year's Eve 2001, we received the devasting news that Simon's cancer had returned. Happy New Year to us!

We were told that Simon needed an intense course of chemotherapy. This made him very sick. He had a pump connected to him which delivered morphine to ease the pain. He received regular visits from a wonderful team of Macmillan nurses, who used to provide him with injections to help ease the sickness.

I was genuinely concerned about how I was going to tell the children about this devasting news. I spoke to the nurses, who brought over some great books that explain cancer in child-friendly language. A very informative one they worked with is called 'The Secret C: Straight Talking About Cancer', by Julie A. Stokes. The nurses were very thoughtful. They also brought Sophie a teddy bear, and they sat with her and her teddy and read her the story, and answered any questions that she had. They spoke to her in detail about the bad cells in Daddy's body.

We were very fortunate that a few months before Simon actually died, we went to Disneyland in Paris. It was before his chemotherapy had finished, but as he was having a good few weeks, we decided to go. My mother-in-law also came with us. Simon got tired very quickly and we hired a wheel chair. We have many photos and videos from the trip, which is a lovely memory.

15

When we returned home unfortunately Simon contracted Septicaemia and his condition really deteriorated. He passed away a couple of months later.

Before Simon died, I was living in fear. I was terrified about how I would live without my husband, my best friend, my soulmate and my children's father. How would I cope with a very challenging son, how would I live on my own? Then I got that dreaded phone call. It was all so surreal. I immediately felt totally shocked and overwhelmed.

I had the perfect marriage and life, and then I lost it all. Just like that. I just felt totally broken, overwhelmed and grief stricken. I was very vulnerable and what I was going through felt like an endless ordeal. I was so stuck through that period and thought I would never see the light again.

A wonderful quote that really does sum up how much he meant to all of us is:

"To the world he was one, to us he was the world"

How Simon's Dear Friends Remember Him

The letters in this chapter were received from dear friends of Simon's, expressing how they felt about him as a person and sharing their fond memories of him being in their lives. I would like to express my heartfelt gratitude and say thank you to each of them for the comfort they brought me and my family.

My earliest recollection of Simon was in the 6th form at Wanstead high school, the chemistry lab. We were all doing a classroom experiment heating up a test tube full of liquid with a Bunsen burner. Simon must have accidentally tapped his test tube on the burner as it cracked and the liquid ended up all over his trousers. As we looked down towards Simon's legs his trousers started melting in front of our eyes, falling apart into synthetic shreds. He was forced to pull them off quickly before his legs were burnt, and with very rosy cheeks the embarrassed Simon had to walk out of school in his underpants and drive home to get new trousers for the next lesson.

We became very friendly and would meet up regularly to play board games such as Risk and Monopoly. Simon was not overly competitive; he enjoyed the banter and the social get-together. He also went to the local clubs with a group of us, where he expanded his social group. We even persuaded Simon to go on a skiing vacation with a group of local friends, which he survived and thoroughly enjoyed. Another year Simon, his brother Barry, Doug (a uni friend of mine) and I went on an amazing road trip around North America and Canada. That was where we learned Simon had a phobia of spiders and snakes. I had a mean streak, and so teased him often.

When Simon first got ill it was a miserable time. He went from hospital to hospital, they could not find the problem, even diagnosing that it was self-induced pain or all in his mind. It was not, and eventually a consultant found the pancreatic cancer which had been growing and spreading for far too long. I do not think it would have made a difference though as that diagnosis is generally a death sentence, with very few people surviving more than five years. They had to remove so many of Simon's internal organs where the cancer had spread including the pancreas, stomach, and intestines. Incredibly Simon recovered and lived an amazing near normal life for many years. Even though he returned every year for check-ups and had to take many medications for the rest of his life. He even met and married the love of his life, Sharon, with whom he went on to have two lovely amazing children, Sophie and Oliver, whom he was very proud of. Simon also had a great career working as a pharmacist and manager at Boots the Chemist, so it seemed like a fairy tale ending. But this was not to be. They didn't live happily ever after.

Unfortunately after 14yrs Simon fell ill again. Much to his surprise, he thought it was all behind him after all this time, but the doctors confirmed the cancer had returned and that they were amazed he had gone on for so long in remission.

That was why they had recalled Simon every year. They knew it was just a matter of time. But Simon had miraculously gone on for many more years than 99% of other pancreatic cancer patients. This was a shock to Simon, but reality set in and Simon sort of knew the clock was ticking. Towards the end when the pain had returned and he was fitting, I seem to recall, he was finally taken into Whips Cross hospital for the last time. He informed me that he had signed a non-resuscitation form. He still felt it wasn't close to the end, and was quite perky considering. Then a junior doctor attended him and told him that they felt he only had hours remaining. This really disturbed and upset Simon. When his mother arrived she had to console him and to accept the reality herself. She was very brave. She then proceeded to have a real go at the doctors telling them they need to learn to speak to these people with compassion and understanding and not to be so blunt and ruthless. Even doctors can have a lack of common sense. Nevertheless Simon went into a coma which he did not return from.

We haven't forgotten Simon. I still visit him now and then. Sometimes I come across photos of us. This gentle, kind and considerate young boy whom life had dealt bad cards made the most out of life and left us all with lovely memories.

Farrell Bently

****

I first had the privilege of meeting Simon in 1979, during our first term of us both studying pharmacy at Chelsea College in London.

In subsequent years Simon never failed to embarrass me by relating, to whoever would listen, that during that first encounter I had asked him if he was Jewish. With the surname Rosenbloom and an address in Ilford, I should have known better. But if the future self-consciousness I experienced was the price I paid for our long-term friendship, then it was a small one to pay.

Throughout and after university we continued as buddies and I remember being invited to Simon's 21st birthday bash at no less a venue than the Savoy Hotel in London. It is still the one and only time I have been there for a function.

Although we worked for different employers we saw each other as often as we could. Simon's great love was cars and I remember him purchasing a Nissan GT with a 2.8 litre engine – something I could only aspire to.

In 1986 I met my beautiful wife yet we still continued to go out, often as a threesome. A visit to a Southend casino and a hearty slap-up meal afterwards proved to be our favourite form of entertainment. Later that year I became engaged (not to Simon!) and even at the party it was evident that Simon was far from well. He started receiving treatment a short time later and it is a source of constant regret that Simon was unable to attend our wedding the following year as he was undergoing treatment in hospital. Simon subsequently went into a cycle of remission and treatment and it was during that time that, for me, he achieved his greatest goal by meeting and subsequently marrying his beloved wife Sharon and fathering two beautiful children, Sophie and Oliver.

The world is a poorer place without Simon. May his dear soul rest in peace.

Barry Sonenfield

****

I first met Simon in the mid-80s. We both worked at Boots the Chemist, he was a newly qualified pharmacist and I was doing my pre-registration year, sort of like an apprenticeship before you are licensed to practise. Simon 'took me under his wing' and we became friends. Simon was a kind, gentle person, very considerate and close to his mum, as well as a really good pharmacist and Boots Manager. Simon was also very determined and driven once he set his mind to do something, be that losing weight (he must have lost about 5 stone in a few months) or buying a new flat.

Outside work, he loved his Ford Capri at the time, and we used to joke that he saw himself as the Martin Shaw character from The Professionals. Neither of us had girlfriends at that time and we spent quite a bit of time together in the late 80s hanging out and chilling as they say now. We also played quite a lot of golf. I was rubbish but Simon was even worse, though he never gave up trying. Simon had an impact on people's lives even beyond the intended. I remember once he was set up on a blind date and arranged for his date to bring another girlfriend so that I could come too. Even though it didn't work out, I introduced his date to another close friend and they ended up getting married.

Simon also persuaded me to do an MBA, which we started together with the Open University. I am eternally thankful for him for this, although this is one of the only things he never completed, it gave me the impetus to change careers once I had finished, as I always disliked pharmacy.

Simon is long gone but not forgotten. I often think about him and what he might have been doing now had the dice fallen differently. His legacy is carried on by Sharon and his two children, but he touched so many people including me and I know my life is better for having known him.

Julian Greene

****

PART 1. How I met Simon

It was January 1985 and Simon's brother, Barry – the dentist – was anchoring onto one of my molars, preparing for extraction, when he asked: "Michael, could you do me a favour?" "Uggghhh!" I replied.

"Thanks," he said, "I believe you are going on the same ski trip to Andorra, in March, as my brother Simon is. Could you look after him please?"

March came along and, as we were getting on the coach, Simon came over and introduced himself.

Simon was a rubbish skier. He hated it before he even got on the snow. He hated the boots, he hated the chairlift, he hated falling over and he did that a lot on the first day!

The second day Simon decided skiing wasn't for him and stayed in the hotel! Luckily for Simon, on the third day (of a two week holiday) I had a skiing accident and dislocated my shoulder. So that was the end of my skiing for that trip.

Then, on day four, while everyone else was out skiing, Simon took control, taking me to the various local cafes and bars and introduced me to his world...arcade games! Simon loved them; he was really good at them. Not only was I crap, I only had one useful hand, so I preferred to watch him.

In between the gaming, we went for walks and chatted and I got to know the quiet, modest, authentic gentleman that Simon was. There wasn't a pretentious bone in his body. He was intelligent, understated, and almost apologetic in his manner. He told me that, although he was a confident manager of a large Boots Pharmacy, he was shy in social situations and especially with the opposite sex.

After that holiday, Simon and I became good friends. We met up at least once a week and I would always drag him along to parties and events at the weekend to try to help him overcome his social awkwardness. As soon as we arrived at a party, he would head straight for a chair and root himself to it. I would set him little challenges such as: "Simon, I am going to circulate for 10 minutes. When I get back, I want to see you talking to that girl over there or be at the bar fixing a drink. After ten minutes, when I returned, Simon was still sitting on the same chair with a gentle smile on his face. I decided then, it was my mission to get Simon laid! Little did I know then!

Part 2. Simon, pre Sharon.

Simon was a polite and obliging gentleman. He was also a mummy's boy and proud of it. He liked living at home. He had his mum, Estelle. He had his friends and, above all, he had his MS Flight Simulator 4 computer game.

When Estelle sold the house and moved into a flat, Simon took the opportunity to buy his own place. He acquired a beautiful cottage and, in so doing, he also acquired his independence.

Even though Simon did not appear to have a mirror in the cottage, he was always well groomed in his standard dress of t-shirt and jogging bottoms or jeans. His smile was ever-present and his outdoor pursuits included golf and his Ford Capri.

Simon and I shared mutual friends and, in addition, he introduced me to one or two of his other friends. Simon made a lot of good friends, thanks to the Ski Group. Because Simon wasn't a confident mixer, he struggled to socialise at parties and therefore romance remained elusive.

Then Simon got sick. He developed pancreatic cancer and spent a year of his life in Hammersmith Hospital. Everyone rallied round him and we all managed a rota so that he was visited regularly. We clubbed together and got him a portable TV as they didn't have bedside TV's in those days. When Simon finally left hospital (minus his pancreas) he was diabetic. Even then his Dunkirk spirit showed through. He just got on with it, even showing those of us who were curious, how his epi-pen worked.

In restaurants, when there was a long queue, Simon would boldly march up to the maître d' and explain he was diabetic and needed to eat immediately and get us fast-tracked to a table.

Socially, Simon seemed content. He had friends, he had hobbies, he had a good job and he had independence. I realised then that Simon didn't need the crassness of my original mission. Simon needed to be in a relationship!

Part 3. The Date.

So, my friend Simon had one thing missing in his life - apart from a pancreas. It was the love of a good woman. And it was my mission to rectify this situation.

I mentioned this to my girlfriend at the time, Ruth. Ruth had a friend, her name was Sharon. Like Simon, Sharon worked in a pharmacy. Like Simon, she had also recovered from cancer and, like Simon, Sharon was looking for a meaningful relationship with a decent member of the opposite sex. A blind date was arranged!

When I told Simon, he was nervous. But I knew he was excited because he combed his hair twice that week.

The week must have dragged slowly for Simon. It did for me! Then finally, the big night finally arrived. Ruth and I agreed we would bring our respective 'candidates' directly to the restaurant to avoid any embarrassment or discomfort that may have occurred if we had all gone in one car.
The evening that Sharon and Simon met is a blur. I seem to remember Ruth and I did most of the talking. Simon sat there

with a pleasant smile on his face but, as he was not an overly animated or talkative individual, his mouth stayed shut for the most part and Ruth and I couldn't gauge whether Simon was enjoying the evening or if Sharon would even be interested in seeing him again.

Then, catastrophe happened. Sharon accidentally knocked a glass of Coke over Simon! Ruth and I thought that was that. The evening ended and Ruth left with Sharon.

In the car on the way home, I asked Simon what he thought. "I liked her," he said. Sharon told Ruth that she liked Simon, too. Sharon's phone number was duly passed to Simon. And the rest is history! ☺

Michael Silverstone

****

I met Simon when we were on the same skiing trip in the 1980s when 20 to 30 friends got together each year to visit a different ski resort. Simon was easy going, moulded in with everybody and a likeable person.

I remember visiting Simon at the Marsden Hospital in 1987/8 when he was diagnosed with cancer. I recall a group of friends clubbed together to get Simon a portable television for him to watch while he was in hospital. Simon always had a positive attitude with a smile on his face. As many friends do, in time, we had our own lives and went our own way but I found out from another mutual friend that Simon had Cancer again.

When I found out that Simon had passed away, I went to see Sharon when she was sitting Shiva (in mourning). I introduced myself as we hadn't met before and told Sharon how I knew Simon and that I was in the process of moving from Bushey back to this neighbourhood. Sharon said that when I moved back to get in contact, which I did. At that time, we became close friends and the rest is history!

I am very proud how Sharon has explored many things that she would never have previously tried or tested but I feel she has rediscovered herself. You deserve to do well with your lovely family.

Love Elizabeth Xx

****

In memory of Simon who was such a gentle soul, with a humorous, warm and kind personality. He is still greatly missed.

Debra Graham

My First Few Weeks Alone...

I do believe I was functioning on autopilot when Simon died, as I was in denial and I didn't want to believe that he would never be coming back.

I basically hated the world. I hated seeing couples together and always used to think why are they happy, in a relationship, while I am a widow with two young children. Why? Why? Why?

Oliver's disability meant that he attended a special needs school. He used to get picked up by bus every morning, but I never had an exact time of pick-up. It was just anytime from 7.30am. So, we had to be ready and waiting at the door as they did not ring the doorbell or hoot. I just had to be ready and they were frequently up to an hour late.

As soon as he was picked up, I would take Sophie to school. That was the part that I hated doing the most. When I got to her school and parked my car, and people saw me coming, they would often cross the road to avoid me. That used to really upset me and make me angry.

It did not happen with all my friends, and I can now understand why. Many people cannot handle it if you are grieving and just start crying. I suppose all I wanted was a hug and to be told that it is okay not to be okay.

Shopping was another extremely hard time for me. When I saw people that I knew in the supermarket, they would quicky walk up a different aisle to avoid bumping into me. When I got home from the supermarket and unpacked my shopping, there were always things that I used to buy for Simon, and that would start me crying again. I used to throw the things against the wall and scream.

I lived for so long in fear and sadness, I resented families who I felt were a perfect family, with a husband, wife and child. I felt very envious of them and also so very sad for Sophie and Oliver, who had friends with a mum and a dad. I do not know if, at the time, Sophie felt that way, but I certainly did.

No Right Or Wrong Way To Grieve

Stages of grief

There are many stages that you go through while grieving the loss of a loved one. Psychiatrist Elizabeth Kubler-Ross said there are five stages: denial, anger, bargaining, depression and acceptance.

Other psychiatrists say there are seven stages, some say ten and even twelve.

There is neither a right nor a wrong way to grieve. We are all unique, and everyone's journey is different.

These are the twelve stages of grief that I experienced.

1. Shock – We all go into shock and feel totally numb when we lose a loved one. The timing of the shock varies with each individual, whether the death was sudden or expected. Shock sometimes gives us time to absorb what has happened.
2. Grief is universal and we all have a unique experience.
3. Depression – grievers suffer from depression and loneliness in different intensities. Being alone need not result in loneliness.
4. Grief can be harmful to our health – the emotional and mental upset of a loss can cause physical suffering and weakness to illness.

5. Grievers are still normal. Your future looks very uncertain. Life becomes very fearful. You may want to run from life, avoid people and decline new things. You need to be patient with yourself and the process.

6. Guilt – many people blame themselves after the death of a loved one. Maybe for the death itself or for faults in the relationship. A trusted counsellor can help with dealing with guilt feelings.

7. Anger – anger is very natural in grief. People ask: Why? Why him? Why now? Why me? Why like this? There isn't an answer to these questions. We also want to blame someone for the loss: God, doctors, clergy, ourselves, even the loved one who has died.

8. Emotional troubles – the emotions that you suffer may seem overwhelming. By talking to a bereavement therapist, you can work through your thoughts and feelings beneficially.

9. Lack of purpose and direction – we prefer to daydream about what was, or daydream and imagine about what might have been. At this stage, showing gratitude for the past assists in a quicker passing through this stage.

10. Recovery from the death of a loved one takes more than time. It takes a lot of pain and sadness.

11. Healing brings hope – grieving can take time and effort, but slowly hope returns. You can voice your emotions without saying sorry or without embarrassment. You can treasure memories. You begin to show a concern for others. In time, you may

acquire your own ability. It took me many years to fully heal my own life, and to find joy and happiness again.

12. Choose life and accept – eventually you understand that the grief has changed you, but not destroyed you. You can discover new things about yourself and build on strengths that have been developed through your suffering. You can face the future with confidence because life is worth living.

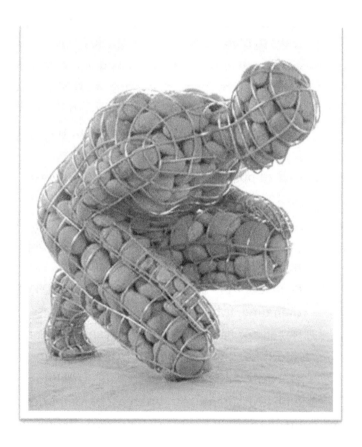

My Journey

In the very early stages of finding myself a widow and a single parent, I was totally overwhelmed and in denial. I was so shocked. I just didn't want to believe that Simon, my husband, my best friend, my soulmate and my world, was gone forever and never coming back. I felt totally numb and disconnected from the world. It was like being in thick, dark fog and you cannot see what is in front of you or how you can get out.

I was really fortunate that I had great support from my mother-in-law Estelle. She was like a rock to me during this time. She had also lost her husband at the early age of forty-nine.

One thing she did advise me to do, which I didn't agree with her about, was not to cry in front of the children. Over the years, I have also seen many clients who have also not cried in front of their children, and they found their children hid their grief.

I always cried together with Sophie and Oliver. I was always very honest with them. I feel that if I had hidden my emotions and feelings from them, they would have hidden their true feelings from me too. They would not have wanted to upset me or make me feel sad. It was important to me to talk about it with them, to honour Simon to ensure we keep him alive in our hearts.

During the first few months, Sophie was worried that she would forget Simon. She didn't want to forget how he looked or how he spoke.

One of the things I used to do with Sophie, when she returned to school, was write down in a notebook how I was feeling and what I had done during the day. I also drew little pictures in the notebook. Sophie would do the same and we'd share what we'd written with each other.

When we had dinner in the evening, Oliver used to constantly want to talk while we were talking, and we tried to take it in turns to talk about how our day was. He still does this now and it was difficult for Sophie and me to have a conversation together on our own.

Sophie, I want you to know that I love you unconditionally, and I am so sorry I haven't always been able to give you the time you deserve and needed.

It was very different with Oliver. His psychotherapist said that it could take about three years before he started to grieve. Every day, Oliver would ask me, 'when is daddy coming ding dong?', which in Oliver's language was 'when is daddy coming home?'. Every day, he said that to me. It felt like another knife being stabbed a bit deeper into my heart and twisted around.

I just used to say to him, 'Daddy died and he won't be coming home.' I just could not stop myself from crying. Oliver never understood the word 'died'. He would then ask me why I was sad and I had to tell him again.

Anger

After a month or so, I felt that I was totally consumed with anger. I was angry with the world, including Simon. I was angry with him for leaving me on my own, and for leaving me with two young children, one of whom was very challenging. I was angry that he would not see the children pass all their achievements at school, he would not see Sophie graduate from university if she went, and he would not be able to walk her down the aisle when she got married.

I was angry with the medical team who were taking care of Simon, as I wondered why didn't he have chemotherapy when he was first diagnosed with his cancer fourteen years previously.

I was angry with my family too, as many upsetting issues had gone on during this time. I remember a week before Simon died, when he was in the hospice, I really needed my mum's help, and asked her to come over and support us to look after Sophie and Oliver. Unfortunately, it was not convenient as she had an appointment. I would have understood if it was urgent but, sadly, it was not. It was an appointment to have her nails done.

35

The following week, when I reluctantly asked for her support again, to come round on the day Simon died, she had a different appointment. This time, she was having her hair done. My mother-in-law Estelle really lost it with my mum due to these decisions she made at the time. There were some terrible rows as a consequence of all this.

Even in families who are very close, during such painful times like grief, there are usually fallouts and disagreements with loved ones.

I was extremely angry and upset with the Synagogue and the Rabbi. I had phoned them about a week before Simon died as he wanted to meet the Rabbi before he actually passed away. My call went to voice mail, I left a message on the answering machine saying that my husband was terminally ill and would it be possible for the Rabbi to phone us. The Rabbi returned my call three weeks later, but Simon had sadly died. I was very rude to him and basically told him where he could go, and I hung up on him.

During the grieving process, many people find a great comfort in their religion, but others like me lose their faith and beliefs. I used to think that if there is a God, why did he take my wonderful husband, especially as there are so many evil people in the world. I felt that life was very unfair.

I was angry with Sophie's school over an incident. Simon's Macmillan nurse had given Sophie a book that explains cancer to children. The book is called 'The Secret C: Straight Talking about Cancer', by Julie A. Stokes.

Sophie wanted to take the book to school so that it could be read to the class, to share with her friends and classmates to help them to understand what was happening in her life. I wrote a letter to the school to request that the teacher issue a letter to the parents requesting their consent – to ensure it was agreeable with everyone for their child to be in the class while the story was read out to them. That sadly did not happen, and the school neglected to obtain the parents' consent. Some children went home and told their parents they were read a book about cancer and dying. As a consequence, I had to endure a lot of gossiping about our family from the parents, especially as some of them would not even say the word 'cancer' to their children at this time. My life was made so much more difficult by that incident. As if it wasn't hard enough taking Sophie to school every day.

I personally do feel it is better to be honest with children rather than make up a story that is not true. When I was a child, if my parents were ever talking about anyone who was unwell, if they had cancer or had unfortunately died from cancer, they would always say the 'C word'. Because of this, I always had such a fear of cancer, as it was something that I did not feel you should talk about.

People will always be angry with someone or something while they are grieving. It is part of a horrible process we must go through.

Be willing to feel your anger even though it may seem endless.

When you truly start to feel it, the more it will disperse and the more you will heal, said Psychiatrist Elizabeth Kubler-Ross.

Guilt

I then felt guilty over so many things. I felt guilty for being the one still here and felt that Simon deserved to be here more than I did. I felt guilty for being both a mum and a dad to my children, as I felt they deserved more than I could give them. I felt guilty for crying all the time and not letting Simon talk about his feelings to me before he died.

On a positive note, on Father's Day each year, Sophie always used to also get me a card.

The first Father's Day after Simon died, her card said: "To a very special friend."

When I opened it up, she had written:

To mummy
What can I say, you are amazing. You are like both a
mummy and daddy to me. And I thank you so very
much, you are the best in every single way. I love you
so very very much.
Loads and loads and loads of love and kisses
From Sophie x

Reading that card always makes me feel emotional, and it also fills me with so much love and gratitude.

There will always be certain dates that can bring you crashing down, even when you have gone through the grieving process.

For me personally, it is always hard on Simon's birthday, the anniversary of his death, Father's Day and our wedding anniversary. Every year, they make me more aware of how much I am missing my Simon.

There are always songs that make me feel very emotional. One in particular is Stevie Wonder's 'I just called to say I love you', as Simon often used to sing that to me when he called. I remember once being in a very busy lift not long after Simon died when that song came on and I just burst into tears.

There is an excellent film about emotions called 'Inside Out'. It's a Disney film, which is so good to watch with kids. What I got from it was, however dark and painful things get and feel,

39

you can always shift your focus and, in time, you will find joy and happiness.

It may seem impossible at the time, but if you look at the spelling of impossible, it says 'I'm possible', so if you keep fighting and pushing yourself, you will eventually see a shift.

There will be many bumps and fall downs along the way. It's like being on a very fast rollercoaster. However sad, angry, frustrated, guilty or fearful you may be feeling, feel it and then let it pass. When you feel it, you release it and let it flow.

I do believe that trapped or suppressed emotions in the body can cause dis-ease, which is when the body is not at ease. I will talk more about this in a later chapter.

But once the emotions are released, you can find joy and happiness. Grief is like the ocean. It comes in waves. Sometimes the water is calm, and sometimes it is so choppy, it overwhelms you. We all have imaginary armbands and have to learn to swim through the ocean and the storm.

Counselling and Therapies

In the beginning, when Simon finally received his diagnosis, I was just crying all the time. Simon, who was a pharmacist, suggested that I go to the doctor and ask for a prescription for anti-depressants, as me being upset all the time was really pulling him down.

The doctor put me on Prozac and Simon's Macmillan nurse suggested that I also see a therapist at the hospice where Simon went. I had an initial assessment first and was seen in about six weeks. The sessions were unlimited and I used to have one session every week. The therapy was reviewed every couple of months and I had therapy for nearly two years.

Simon's employer, Boots, supplied a lovely counsellor for Simon to see and she used to come to us at home once a week. I would go out for an hour to give them the space and time to talk.

Sophie also had a bereavement therapist from school who used to come and see her at home for an hour each week before Simon died. At her school, there was also a lovely lady called Pamela, who was the Welfare Officer. She had also lost her mum to pancreatic cancer, which enabled them to

41

connect freely. Sophie often used to go to her office and they would talk and draw pictures together.

After Simon's death, I decided it was best for Sophie to stay at home for a while to come to terms with the loss of her father. After a little while, she eventually returned to school part-time as I thought she would be better off with her friends. Whenever Sophie got upset, she would go to Pamela's office and they would do some drawing and painting together. We used to laminate her pictures and take them to Simon's grave to share the moments together.

Sophie used to work with a book called 'Muddles, Puddles and Sunshine', by Diana Crossley. It offers practical and sensitive support for bereaved children. It is beautifully illustrated and it suggests a helpful series of activities and exercises, accompanied by the friendly characters of bee and bear. This book offers a wonderful structure and an outlet for the many difficult feelings which inevitability follow when someone dear to you dies. It provides a balance between remembering and having fun. This book is a useful tool in the present and will become an invaluable keepsake in the years to come for children.

I believe the charity that this came from is called 'Winston's Wish'. Sophie also made a memory jar which was filled with coloured sand. The jar was made of glass, and different coloured sand was added, with each colour representing a special memory she had of Simon.

Sophie also made a memory box and kept memorable items in it. She also saw a play therapist at the hospice.

During the first month after Simon's passing, we had some group therapy at the hospice with other families who had lost their husband, wife or partner. The children did some art together and the adults talked about their losses and cried together. It was such a supportive outlet to talk to other people who had also lost their partner at a young age. We all sat around in a circle and, one by one, we shared our experiences of our loss. In the final session, we all let off some helium balloons and we wrote messages on them to our loved ones.

When it was Simon's first birthday after he died, I thought that it would be a nice thing to do with Sophie and Oliver. There is a park opposite where I live. I bought three helium balloons, and Sophie and I wrote messages on them. Then we went to the park to let them off. I said to Oliver that we were going to go to the park for Daddy's birthday. When we got there, he started looking for Simon. I had to try and explain to him what we were doing and he had a complete meltdown. So, a difficult day was made that much harder, trying to find the right words to explain all of this to Oliver.

Oliver's psychotherapist said he probably would not grieve for about three years, and that is exactly how long it took for him. Oliver got a place to see a play therapist at the hospice where Simon died. She was fantastic with Oliver in getting him to understand what had happened.

One of the first things she did was to take a photo of Simon and put some tracing paper over the photograph and draw an outline of him. Then she flipped it up and explained that Simon's soul had left his body, as his body did not work anymore.

I was not sure if Oliver really understood what she was doing but I do feel this technique would be excellent for mainstream children experiencing a loss.

Then they played with dolls. Each week she spoke to Oliver about Daddy not being well and having special medicine to try and make him better. Then eventually she explained that Daddy was too ill and he died. The doll was put in a box and buried in a sandpit. She then recommended that I take him to the cemetery where Simon was, which was another challenge for me.
So although I had finished my counselling, I felt like I went backwards and had to go through it all over again with Oliver some years later.

Some people find it difficult to cry, especially men, as their narrative may be 'big boys don't cry', or 'don't be a cry baby, or be strong'. I do believe that you become stronger if you do cry and release your feelings.

There are many different types of therapies available and I do believe that an integrated approach is the best.

I had Person Centred Therapy, which is exceptionally good for bereavement, and there is also Cognitive Behavioural Therapy and Psychodynamic Therapy. These I will talk about more in another chapter.

I like to use an integrated approach with my clients, which uses a combination of all the techniques. I find them immensely beneficial as everyone is unique, and everyone's grief journey will be different.

Also life coaching is very helpful when you reach the acceptance stage to help you move forward with your life.

Art therapy is also very helpful, especially if you find it difficult to talk. Both art therapy and play therapy are excellent for children.

I do believe it is imperative that you find a therapist who is empathic, non-judgemental, open, warm and trustworthy. Someone who you feel you can be honest with about how you are actually feeling.

Hiding From Grief

It is exceedingly difficult to know how to deal with grief, and to be with the deep sadness and overwhelm of the emotions that you are feeling. We try to draw away from it, to hide and escape from it. Many people learn this sort of behaviour from their parents and how they handled grief. People are often told 'to put on a brave face'. I do believe that a brave face is just a mask covering the deep pain and emotions you are really feeling.

Many people are taught to ignore, deny and look for a quick fix solution such as food, alcohol, drugs or shopping.

I do believe now, after doing a lot of work on myself, that by being on anti-depressants for eight years, I was partially hiding my grief.

Every three months, I used to put in for a repeat prescription and I used to just get it. I was never actually seen by the doctor for a check-up. I was so scared of coming off them as I did not know how I would cope alone without Simon. They kept me in a safe bubble rather than me actually feeling the pain from my grief or dealing with it.

I was on anti-depressants for far too long, but I feel it was cheaper for the doctor to keep me on them rather than deal with the issue, which would have been to refer me to another therapist or to give me some help with Oliver.

There is a homeopathic remedy called Ignatia, which is excellent in the early stages of grief.

Many people turn to excess drug taking, alcohol, smoking or excess food consumption when they go through the grief cycle. Two big addictions for me personally were food and shopping. Eighteen years down the line, I am now addressing this with my thoughts and feelings. I have a fantastic mentor/trainer, Chris Hill.

Chris Hill unfortunately lost his twin brother to a drug overdose, and for over twenty years, he also struggled with many different addictions. He enables clients to beat any addictive activity or change any negative thoughts, feelings and emotions.

Facing Challenges Alone

Grief is the darkest, heaviest and most challenging emotion you will ever have to go through.

My whole life was completely shattered. How was I going to live without Simon, my husband, my soul mate, my best friend and my children's father. How was I going to look after the children on my own, how was I going to look after the household things and how was I going to sort out any financial affairs?

I just didn't want to be here on my own. The pain was so deep, and I just felt totally shattered as if my life had been broken into a million tiny pieces. How would I ever be able to fix it?

Too painful to answer the telephone

The phone would often ring and I wouldn't answer it until I knew who was calling, as I found it too painful to speak to many people, especially friends of Simon's. It took me just over seventeen years to eventually phone Julian back, who was one of Simon's closest friends, who kindly shared a letter previously mentioned in my book.

Simple DIY at home

I remember one day being in the kitchen on my own and a light bulb blew. My first thought was that Simon will take care of that when he gets home. Then a second later, I realised he will never be able to do a simple job like change a light bulb again, and I just broke down in that moment and could not stop crying.

I knew a few days before Simon actually died that it would only be a matter of days, before he would leave us.

Taking cloths to a charity shop
I actually took all his clothes to the cancer research charity shop. So many clients that I have seen over the years find this process so difficult to do. I knew that if I waited until after he had died, I would not be able to do it. Every time I went past the shop, I had to cross the road and I was always scared to look in the window in case I saw any of his things. Maybe it would have been better if I had taken them to an area where I did not shop.

Going to events alone

Going to events alone for me was a definite no-no. A few months after Simon died, I had a friend's son's bar-mitzvah to go to, but I just could not go on my own. I could not face sitting round a table with eight other couples, with me on my own. Some people said I should go as it would be good for me to go out. But how could I possibly go without my Simon?

My friends would often invite me over for dinner, but I just did not want to go out alone. The thought of sitting at the dinner table and not having my Simon with me was too painful. If only I could have one more day, one more hour, one more minute with him!

Grief is one of the heaviest emotions you ever have to carry.

Dealing with paper work

I found it so difficult every day when the post came and letters were addressed to Simon. After several months, I filled out a form and sent it off with his death certificate, and the majority of the post stopped. But even now, eighteen years down the line, I still receive the odd random letter. I have never found a way to stop random phone calls asking for Simon.

I was fortunate that we had time before Simon died to get all the utilities transferred into my name, and the same with our joint bank accounts.

As I was the only adult living in my home, my council tax was reduced by 25%.

I had to send his driving licence back to the DVLA and return his passport. These are all very challenging life tasks to complete when you lose a loved one.

Coming to terms with my fears

I was totally living in fear. I was fearful of absolutely everything. I live opposite a park which is a shortcut into the village, but I would not go into the park on my own as I was so scared.

It was also a much quicker way for Sophie to go to school, but I would not let her walk through the park. One day she did and I saw her do it, and I grounded her for a week. Thank goodness my fears did not rub off on her.

I do believe that my fear came from my past beliefs growing up as a child, learnt unconsciously from my parents, that it was not safe to walk through the park on my own. Now I feel that if I am being fearful maybe it would attract something that is fearful to me.

Of course, it is safe to walk through the park, and even safer now that I am not living in fear. Now when I walk through the park, I smile at other people and acknowledge them, safe in the knowledge that fear is my choice, I get to decide if I live in fear or not.

Widowedwithkids.co.uk

Energy Healing

A beautiful lady that I met at my first Anna Garcia event is called Gozi Halima. She is an energy healer, coach and a Theta healer.

I didn't actually know what energy healing was and these are Gozi's words to me.

"We are solely responsible for our lives as we are the ones creating our reality. However, most of this creation is happening unconsciously and is heavily influenced by our inherited or environmental programming, which accounts for over 90 percent of what we do. Through energy work we can start breaking down any limiting patterns or behaviours that occur in the 90 percent so that you can start living a more empowered and joyful life consciously."

We can re-wire our subconscious mind with new positive programmes and influence 90% of our actions and emotions. This is because our conscious mind is only responsible for about 10% of our actions and the other 90% is all our subconscious.

I lived in total fear, I didn't love myself, I didn't have confidence, I didn't trust myself, I didn't think I was worthy, and I had so many limiting beliefs.

Limiting beliefs are things that you believe about yourself that place limitations on your life. They are thoughts in your subconscious that tell you something that is not true.

Things that we say to ourselves manifest in our lives. Our thoughts are powerful as they control our emotions. When we don't believe we can, then we won't.

Examples of the things I used to say all the time include: I can't walk through the park on my own, I can't go on a train on my own, I can't go on an aeroplane on my own, I can't go to a gym or exercise, I can't lose weight, I can't write a book!

When I was about three years old, I got lost in Selfridges one day. And as a child this would have caused PTSD (Post Traumatic Stress Disorder). If when I was found I'd been given a hug and told that I am loved and thank God I am safe, it would have been the end of it. But I was probably told off for being a naughty girl. I do now believe this is why I was always anxious about getting lost or finding new places on my own.

After working with Gozi, I feel I now have freedom and a new lease of life. I have compassion and kindness for myself. My whole life has really transformed.

I remember the first time I went through my local park. I must have been very anxious and nobody was smiling or saying good morning. Then a lovely old man started chatting to me and we walked round the park together. Everyone was saying good morning to him. The following day, I did it again and I said good morning to others and they then said it back to me. So, I do believe my energy has had huge shifts.

I had never been away on my own and after working with Gozi, I connected with an old friend of mine who lives in

Singapore. I decided that I would go and stay with her for a couple of weeks, but unfortunately that got cancelled due to Covid 19.

I did have a bit of weight to release. I have slim arms but I would never wear a sleeveless top. I always wore a cardigan over everything, even in the summer. After one of our sessions in June 2019, I went out with a shirt without sleeves and no cardigan, and I felt so free.

I also believe the reason why I have had difficulty in losing weight is it's another loss. So I now say 'releasing' weight.

I absolutely love the gym now, and exercise is so good for you, especially while you are grieving. Exercise releases dopamine, which is the happy hormone. It doesn't necessarily make you happy, but it gives you a temporary feel-good factor.

I even gave a talk one day at a networking event, about bereavement and life coaching, which was a huge energy shift for me, and I am loving my new growth journey.

Believe that you can and you will!

Gozi helped me to really shift my energy to release so many negative thoughts and beliefs.

You can find out more about Gozi at:

www.gozphilosophy.com

The Importance Of Looking After Yourself

Many people cannot handle grief. Grief is one of the heaviest emotions that you will ever have to deal with. You may not feel like taking care of yourself, as grieving takes all your energy. But you really need to try and take care of yourself, because if you don't look after yourself, how can you take care of and look after your children.

Taking care of yourself does not mean that you are not missing your loved one. I believe it is honouring their memory.

Accept help

Accept help whenever it is offered, because if people think you are coping, they will back away from offering again. So when your friends or family offer you some help, say 'thank you' and accept it. I know it is easier to say 'I'm okay', when you are feeling totally broken inside, but if friends or family offer to look after your children, I would recommend accepting and taking a few hours for yourself, even if it is just to try and get some sleep.

Widowedwithkids.co.uk

If friends or family offer to cook you meals, say 'thank you' and accept it. I lived on takeaways and processed food for far too long.

If people offer to do shopping for you, accept it.

This is a time for healthy eating, exercise, getting enough sleep, and it is imperative to not turn to alcohol or drugs. I personally turned to sugar and shopping. I know now that it used to fill a void in me.

Healing power of exercise

Exercise whenever you can, as exercise releases endorphins in your brain, which are very healing. Fitness is not about your size; it is about the size of your life.

Gentle movement such as walking is valuable and is grounding. If you have any supportive friends who you can talk with, cry with, and who can just be there if you need a hug, invite them to join you.

Journaling

Journaling about your grief, painting or using another form of art is very therapeutic too, and music and dancing are also very helpful to shift your focus. These are great stress reducers and help clear all the negative thoughts in your mind.

Meditating

You cannot stop your feelings and emotions, and deep breathing or meditating and journaling your thoughts really helps to get all your thoughts out of your head. It took me seventeen years to get into meditating and when I first started doing it, my mind said 'I can't do this' and I stopped. I now meditate every day and sometimes twice a day, and it really helps to clear my mind. I use a meditation app called 'Headspace'.

Hydration

Drinking plenty of water is imperative, because if you have been crying a lot, it will help to rehydrate you, and it will also help to flush toxins from your body. I never really used to drink much water and I suffered from so many headaches. Nearly every day, I had a headache and always used to take pharmaceutical drugs. All I needed was to drink some water as my body was so dehydrated.

Say their name

Always say your loved one's name. Other people may feel uncomfortable saying their name around you, but I would say things like 'Simon used to love doing that', or 'that was Simon's favourite food', or 'Simon didn't like that', etc.

Stay true to yourself

Do not judge yourself or compare yourself to others.
Life is a journey. Unfortunately, I had to go through the darkest time of my life at a young age, and now I have been given the opportunity to find out who I really am, and why I am here.

It does not matter how others perceive me, what is important is how I perceive myself.

Connect with yourself every day. It took me about six to eight months to fully get this, but listen to how are you actually feeling each day. It is important to write down each day in a journal all your feelings.

Write down any negative thoughts you have in a journal. Once it is written down, it is out of your head.

Believe you can and you are halfway there.

Change is an opportunity for growth, embrace it and do not try to resist it.

You cannot stop the pain that you are feeling, but there are ways you can reduce it.

If you think you cannot, you will not. If you think you can, you will.

You cannot stop your feelings and emotions, but deep breathing and meditating and journaling your thoughts really help to keep your mind free.

Take your time

Grieving is the longest, slowest process you have to go through. Take one day at a time to rebuild your life, and take baby steps. I never want to replace Simon, but I do feel my heart and love can expand when the time is right for me. I choose now to live for both of us.

People may say you are young so move on with your life. That used to really upset me because you never move on, but I do feel that, in time, you do move forward.

Life is difficult, but it is how you respond to your difficulties that matters.

What you can do when you do not feel like doing anything

1. Take a five-minute walk

2. Yoga is good and there is also grief yoga. Yoga is the union of your mind, body and breath.

3. Eat a healthy meal

4. Soak in a hot bath with maybe some essential oils or some Epsom salts.

5. Meditate

6. Journal

7. Read an inspiring book, or listen to one on audio

8. Say your loved one's name, as often as you like, and talk to them

9. Use some essential oils in a diffuser: there are many that are beneficial for emotions.

10. Listen to a podcast

11. Join a grief group on social media

Survival Tips

Talk to friends or family about how you honestly feel about your grief, and don't put on a brave face because you feel that is expected of you or because they want you to be strong or okay. It's okay to not be okay.

See a bereavement counsellor and life coach if you can, as it is often easier to talk to someone who does not know you or anyone in your family. Make sure they are totally non-judgemental, as well as honest, warm, compassionate, empathic and trustworthy.

Everyone is unique and we all grieve differently. If you feel you have a connection with your therapist, that really will help you through your personal grieving process.

Accept any help if it is offered to you, and always ask if you need help.

Regular exercise is very important as it releases dopamine in the brain, which is the feel-good factor.

Yoga is also good to help you relax. Or just a nice soak in a hot bath with maybe some Epsom salts.

Widowedwithkids.co.uk

Writing in a book or journaling exactly what you are feeling in that moment is really helpful. When you write your own thoughts down, they are not staying in your head.

Make a memory box. This is something I would recommend doing with grieving children too, as they can always look through it when they are happy or sad.

Special and memorable dates are always hard, and when Sophie was younger, I always took her out of school and we would do something nice together to remember the day.

Often you will feel like you are in thick, dark fog, or constant rain and thunderstorms. Eventually the sun will shine. At first, it may be only for a minute, but in divine time, the sun will shine and the temperature will be right for you.

Grief is not a sign of weakness or a lack of faith. It is the price of everything you love.

Talking to Children

Children grieve very differently to adults. One minute they can be laughing and joking, and then the next minute they can be really sad. Adults on the other hand are on a very scary, fast rollercoaster that does not seem to stop.

I do believe that honesty is the best policy. Try and be as honest with your children about your loss and your feelings, so they will be honest with you.

You may think you have to be strong in front of your children. But I do believe that showing your emotions will make you a stronger person. And the same works for your children.

My mother-in-law said to Oliver that daddy had gone to heaven, but he never understood that word. She used to point up to the sky and say it is above the clouds. A few years later, we went to Spain and Oliver was looking out of the plane window looking for Simon once we broke through the clouds.

If you tell a young child that daddy has gone to sleep, it can make them scared to go to sleep. If you say daddy was not very well, they may become scared that they will die when they are unwell.

Be prepared to answer whatever questions your children ask and please be as honest as you can.

Keep talking about daddy to them. I have a friend who lost her father when she was about eleven. She was standing at the top of the stairs when she heard her mum say to her grandma that her father had died. I believe the truth was hidden from her and do feel that it is better to be honest with children.

You are the most important adult in your child's life right now. But there are others who may be willing to help you to support and encourage your children through this difficult time. It could be a friend, teacher at school or support worker. Their different experiences with your loved one will help your children to get a more complete, rounded picture of the person he or she was.

Routine can be a great source of comfort for children. Do what you can to stabilise your routines, including your children's bedtime, so that they have a general idea of what to expect from one moment to the next.

You might be tempted to throw yourself and your children back into your 'normal routine' and do things such as get back to work and school as soon as possible. But you should also take it slowly and give your children the freedom to withdraw from social gatherings or activities if they need some space and time to grieve.

Much of what has already happened is beyond your children's control, so make sure you allow them to make their own choices if possible. This can involve simple decisions about what to wear and what to do in their spare time, within reason.

No one is a perfect parent. We all make mistakes. Let yourself off the hook from the start and acknowledge that you are not going to get everything right, but you are going to get better over time at handling all of the things that are now your responsibility.

Depending on the age of the children, below are some suggestions to try that may be helpful for your children.

- Whether to let your children attend the funeral. I do believe it's something you should talk about with the child. I spoke about this in an earlier chapter regarding Sophie.

- It took me a long time to realise this, but Sophie became the adult in our relationship and I became the child. It was challenging to change it back to me being the adult and Sophie being the child. I did have a lot of guilt about this. I feel she missed so much of her childhood, as she had to grow up so quickly.

- It will be more difficult with teenagers, because of their hormones, and teenagers often don't want to talk to their parents. Schools, colleges and universities usually have support available. Try and see if a good friend can support them.

- Share memories together, make a memory box.
- Allow them the time they need to grieve.
- You don't have to do it alone, reach out for help.
- There are many books about grief for children.
- Art and play therapy can help them to express how they are feeling.
- Counselling for adults, teenagers and younger children is so important to help them express how they are feeling.
- Meditation is helpful as we all have on average 60,000 thoughts a day. Meditation helps you to not get stuck with your thoughts.
- Mindfulness is being present to your mental state and journaling your thoughts is another way for releasing them.
- Social media groups may help teenagers, so they don't feel alone
- Winston's Wish is an excellent charity for child bereavement support.

What Not To Say To Someone Who Is Grieving.

After Simon died, I put a lot of photos up of Simon from our trip to Disneyland and my brother said I had made my house into a shrine to Simon. For me, however, having all his photos around was a little bit like he was still with us. I did not tell my brother, but his comment did feel like another knife being put in my heart.

Over the years, I have seen many clients. Some have lots of photos and memorabilia, and others can't even look at their photos as it's too painful. There is no right or wrong way to grieve.

Many people find it difficult to know what to say to someone who is grieving. Below are some of the worst things that people said to me and how they made me feel.

- I know how you feel, I got divorced last year.
My thought was how on earth can you know how I feel, at least your children still have their father.

- Do not cry in front of your children.
  I do not feel that this is a good idea, because if you hide your feelings from your children, they will hide

67

their feelings from you, as they won't want to upset you. I believe honesty is the best policy. Cry together and, if you can, laugh together too.

- I know how you feel, my cat died last month.
  I know for some people their pets are like family to them, and they do go through the grieving process when they die. But for me, I could not see the comparison.

- You're so strong.
  I certainly didn't feel strong, I was just about surviving.

- You're so brave.
  I definitely was not brave. I felt a total failure.

- You're young; you'll meet someone else.
  Yes, I was young. The last thing I wanted was someone else. The only person I wanted was My Simon.

- When you meet someone else, the children will have a new dad.
  They didn't want a new dad. They wanted their Daddy.

- You're so lucky, at least your mortgage has been paid off.
  How on earth could someone say that to me, however much debt they were in.

People say these types of things because they do not know what else to say. For me, personally, if they had just said 'I am sorry' and perhaps given me a hug, or offered some kind of help, that would have been enough.

Other things you could say to someone who is grieving are:

- I am so sorry for your loss.
- I don't know how you feel, but I am here to help in any way I can.
- You and your loved one will be in my thoughts and prayers.
- My favourite memory of your loved one is…
- I am always just a phone call away.
- Give a hug instead of saying something.
- We all need help at times like this, I am here for you.
- I am usually up early or late, if you need anything.
- Saying nothing, just be with the person.

Some people genuinely want to help and support you, although they often are worried that they will say the wrong thing. If you need help, reach out, even if you wouldn't usually ask for help, as your friends and family will most likely be pleased to support you.

Widowedwithkids.co.uk

Addictions

I believe my addictions started when Simon passed away. Whenever I felt angry or sad, which was most of the time, I would comfort eat. I ate more and more chocolate, cakes and junk food rather than anything healthy. Whenever I felt any emotion, and that was the majority of the time, I would just eat, and eat, and eat. I ate more and more chocolate, cakes and junk food rather than actually feel my emotions.

I consequently put on nearly five stone in approximately two years.

I did not want to cook meals for me and the children, so we either got takeaways or ate processed food that I could cook quickly in the microwave.

I filled a massive void with food. Every time I felt sad, my mind would say to me 'have some chocolate'.

During a bereavement, many people eat more or just cannot eat at all. Some people turn to drink, or drugs, or smoking, or shopping, or another addiction.

Eating sugar releases dopamine in the brain, which gives you the feel-good factor for a very short time.

It is the same with alcohol. You drink to block out the pain you are feeling and eventually you become numb from it.

Addiction is when you seek something outside of yourself that can take away the pain, stress or anxiety. You may be afraid that you are not a good person deep down inside. You are running away from problems, and having difficulty living and accepting yourself.

Many people turn to alcohol or drugs. It is the subconscious mind's way of dealing with thoughts and emotions. I believe it's your subconscious mind trying to keep you safe and to protect you.

Studies show that sugar is eight times more addictive than cocaine. A complete overwhelm of the emotions activates the pleasure and reward system in our brains, and releases high levels of dopamine that not even cocaine can compete with.

Dopamine is known as the happy hormone and gives you the feel-good factor. I would eat all the sugary foods and feel goodish for a short time.

It was the same when I went shopping and I bought something new, I got the instant but temporary feel-good factor. Both the sugar and the shopping over the years became addictions for me, which gave me very quick highs. They were a way to increase the dopamine. For years since, I have always had a compulsion with shopping.

Sugar is one of the hardest addictions to give up, as most pre-packaged foods contain some kind of sugar, which gives you the want and need for more.

I followed Chris Hill's programme at beatmyaddiction.com and within 10 days, I was completely sugar free. You do have a couple of bad days on day 4, 5 or 6, but Chris and his team support you through it.

My energy is so much better since I've stopped the sugar. And when I got to day 11, I felt so free.

Chris does the same programme for drugs, alcohol, gambling, smoking, sex, shopping and your negative thoughts.
It took me eighteen years to even know that I had these addictions, and I found Chris Hill by pure chance.

One of my friends asked me if I had heard of Chris Hill, when I was struggling with my weight during Covid-19, and I said no. Then the following day, I was checking my emails and I had an email from him. Was Google listening to us?

When My Life Started To Change

About four years after Simon died, there was an advert in my local paper from a local charity looking for volunteers to do bereavement therapy and this is where my life started to change.

The charity provided a six-week training and I felt that I could offer genuine empathy, trust and unconditional, positive regard. I now help people who are at the darkest and most painful time in their life. I have been with this charity since 2006, and I am now the supervisor.

I then went and did further training, and now I have an advanced Diploma in Counselling, Psychotherapy and Hypnotherapy. I have also completed a Neuro-Linguistic Programming course, life coaching, naturopathy, Reiki, personal development and mindfulness training.

I also completed my placement in a hospice, seeing patients in their final stages of life and also supporting their families during this painful time and afterwards.

Many of my friends asked me how I could be with people who are dying or who are suffering from a bereavement. I feel that this is my way of giving back, as I had a lot of support over the years, and so did Sophie and Oliver, and I have personal experience to share.

I also studied Homeopathy and have two years left to complete my qualification. Homeopathy is completely natural and comes from plants and minerals, and it helps the body in the healing process. What I love about it is when you see a homeopath, you are treated as a whole person and not just your symptoms. A homeopath treats you physically, mentally and emotionally, as everyone is unique. It is totally safe, non-toxic and gentle.

The Homeopathy course is where I felt my seed had been planted, as I now think very differently about conventional medicines. I personally will only use natural medicine now.

A few months before Simon died, I was put on anti-depressants, which did help me at the time, but then I started using them as a crutch as I did not know how I would cope with supporting Sophie and Oliver or managing life on my own.

The anti-depressants kept me in a safe bubble rather than actually allowing me to feel my real pain. I had suppressed so much pain for so many years.

In 2014, I had a very small flat brown mole on my ankle and half was red and lumpy. I went to my GP and she did not like the look of it and referred me to a dermatologist, who removed it. It was a malignant melanoma. I also had some of my lymph nodes removed and then a skin graft.

I personally believe this was due to being on the anti-depressants for so long, as whenever I had any feelings, I always felt them in my ankle. I do feel my body was in dis-ease. Dis-ease means your body isn't at ease.

I personally will always see my homeopath now before going to the GP as I do believe that there are so many side effects from conventional medicines.

New Relationships

After Simon died, I was not actually living or really enjoying my life. I really believe I was just functioning on auto pilot.

I have had two serious relationships since losing Simon, neither of which worked out. I can now see they were both co-dependent and I was trying to fill a massive void in my life.

I do feel that it was because I was not healed 100%. Like attracts like and because I did not love myself, believe in myself or trust myself, my relationships did not work.

What I truly needed was a relationship with myself first. When you can love yourself unconditionally first, then you will be able to love someone else.

This I have come to understand through doing a lot of personal development work.

It is so important to heal yourself first before starting a new relationship, and to learn to love yourself unconditionally, trust yourself, believe in yourself, and not rely on others to fill you up. This is something I did not do, and I learnt the hard way.

I always used to say that I did not want to be sad and lonely on my own. When you can love yourself 100%, you no longer feel alone.

My beautiful friend wrote this poem and when she shared it with me, I said 'Wow!'. This poem seems like it was written for me as it is exactly how I feel now.

Hello Unconditional Love

Hello unconditional love, nice to meet you
I know you have been waiting; patiently for me
To allow you in and receive you
I see you; I feel you
I am breathing you in now
In all your joyful bliss

All love attachments are now dissolved
All fears floated away
The expectations are no more
I am here, sitting with you
Getting to know you, unconditional love
Smiling back at you

Always and forever more, unconditional love
I choose you
I welcome you in to stay
No matter what may flow my way
I embrace you

In all your joyful bliss

Letting you in unconditional love
I know I am worthy
The gift that you are
I am free
Free to be and receive you unconditional love
In all your joy and glory

My life is unfolding
In beautiful ways
In ways one could not have dreamed of
My inner light has shone bright
To bring me home
Home to you unconditional love

By Pippa Mackenzie-Smith

What Made Me Look For Help
Something Needed To Be Different

I was in a relationship that was not working, although I tried my hardest to make it work. One day, I was just scrolling through Facebook when I saw a post from Anna Garcia. Anna is a relationship coach and holds seminars for women only. They are free one-day events where you discover:

1. How to mend your broken heart and trust again.
2. The secret to stop attracting toxic relationships.
3. How to make decisions about your relationship without shame and guilt.
4. How to save a current relationship.
5. The real reason why you are keeping yourself single.
6. The three sure signs that you should leave a relationship now.

And so much more.....

I clicked on the link and Anna called me, and we had a chat and I shed some tears. She told me it was a free event, but if I paid £99, I could attend as a VIP, which is a private group session for women who are ready to shift something on the day and would like to learn how to do so. In the main event, Anna goes through what is going on in your relationships and

79

why. In the VIP session, she goes into how to shift patterns that no longer serve you.

When I asked how many women would be there, she said approximately 150-200. I said there is no way I would stand up and tell my story to that number of people, but I still decided to attend as a VIP.

During the event, Anna asked for a volunteer to share their story. I felt her look at me and my hand shot up. I stood at the mic shaking like a leaf, and I kept saying sorry for everything I said. I said that I wished he would finish with me as I did not want to be the bad one, as he had also lost his wife and he worked with my son at the college he attended.

The event was on the Saturday and the following Wednesday, which was the first day of spring, he finished with me. That was when my life started to change for the better.

Anna also does a mastery programme, which is a three-day event that involves a lot of personal development work. For me, that meant learning to have a relationship with myself, which I had not had for quite a long time.

After doing the first weekend workshop, which I felt I got so much from, I signed up for the year's mastery programme. I now love myself unconditionally, I trust myself, I believe in myself, I have faith in myself and I feel empowered.

*Anna Garcia and I at one of her
incredible events together.*

I Now Feel Life Is For Living Not For Hiding

I spent so many years hiding from myself, and never liked myself in photos. I would always stand at the back or behind someone taller than me if there were any occasions where photos were being taken. Even as a teenager, I always avoided being in photos.

This has come from my limiting belief that I am not good enough, not worthy, and from feeling ugly.

Anna's best friend, Rodney Pedroza, is a portrait photographer. One Saturday at one of Anna's events, Rodney gave me an invitation to have a free photo shoot and have my make-up done.

Rodney Pedroza is a portrait photographer. And a photoshoot with him is not just about pictures, it's about finding yourself through the experience. He first found his love of photography watching his mentor. In that moment, he knew this was what he was meant to be doing for all women.

Over the years, he continued to develop his skills, so that his clients can sparkle even brighter, and when they look in the mirror, they say can these words: 'Hello, you, I love you, and you are perfect the way you are.'

WHY WOULDN'T YOU WANT
TO FALL IN LOVE
WITH THE WOMAN
IN THE MIRROR?

He has an amazing personality and one day he asked me if I was going to go for the photoshoot. I was honest with him and said 'I don't want to waste your time'. I never like myself in photos, and I don't like it when other people do my make-up.

Rodney said I wouldn't be wasting my time, and if I didn't like the make-up, I could remove it and do it myself. I finally decided to give it a go. Even though my ego was saying 'why am I going?'.

The day I was due to go, I got in my car and my sat nav wasn't working. My google maps also weren't working and I got totally lost. I phoned Rodney and he told me how to get to him. My reply was this is the universe telling me not to come. He spoke to me for the rest of the journey until I got to his studio.

And it was definitely an awesome experience. Although even when we had finished, I still thought I wouldn't like the photos when I go back. The only difficulty I had was choosing which ones to have. And then Sharon Rosenbloom transformed into the Rose in Bloom.

'The Secret Language of Your Body' by Inna Segal

When your body is in dis-ease, there is usually a reason why. The next few paragraphs explain the diseases and symptoms that I have suffered over the years. Inna Segal's book describes exactly how I was feeling.

I have had round shoulders and a bad posture for the majority of my life, and after losing Simon, I do believe it got far worse.

However, I have been doing some exercise with a holistic healer (symmetryofmotion.com) and my posture has improved immensely.

Shoulders

I felt like I was carrying the weight of the world on my shoulders. I was holding on to too much strain, stress and worry. I was feeling insecure, unsure, frightened, overwhelmed, sad, rejected, distrustful and discouraged. I was easily hurt. I had droopy shoulders, indicating a lack of joy and fun. My life was all seriousness. I was focusing on problems rather than solutions.

Spine

Feeling week, confused, fearful and insecure. Difficulty communicating with others and asking for what you want. Feeling unsupported and alone. Not knowing who or where to ask for help. Feeling that the world is an unsafe place to live in. Trying to protect yourself from pain and hurt. Feeling stuck in a pattern or situation you can't get out of.

Cervical spine

Feelings of fear, confusion, fight or flight, wanting to run away from problems and responsibilities. Feeling insecure, not good enough, too focused on other people's opinions. Taking on other people's problems.

On the physical level: difficulty sleeping, exhaustion, anxiety attacks due to the effect of negative feelings on the sympathetic nervous system.

Mid spine

Feeling overwhelmed by responsibilities, wanting to run and hide, and let someone else take over. Difficulty letting go and trusting. Inability to love or nurture yourself. Holding on to too much fear and worry, feeling helpless and hopeless, like a victim of your life. Relying too much on the opinions of others, instead of learning to trust and value your own wisdom, inner guidance and intuition.

Feeling stuck, low self-esteem, feeling insecure, fearful and lost. Deep seated belief that you deserve to suffer and struggle. Holding onto guilt from the past, which stops you from moving forward.

Feeling weak, confused, weighed down. As if something is holding you back and you are unable to move forward. A tendency to see yourself as a victim. On the physical level, poor circulation and cold feet.

Sacrum

Feeling unsupported, carrying unresolved family issues, holding onto childhood anger and resentment. Experiencing a lack of confidence and belief in self. Feeling uncomfortable in your body and in your life. Carrying guilt, resentment and shame. On the physical level, spinal curvature.

Balance (loss of)

Feeling unstable, difficulty getting your bearings. Feeling like you are being pulled in different directions.

Brain tumour

In conflict with yourself. Surrounded by negativity and instability, blaming yourself for mistakes from the past. Feeling trapped or out of control without knowing how to change.

Gallstones

Grief that has hardened. Feelings of resentment, irritability, depression. Disappointment about your achievement in the world. Either holding back or exploding with anger. Feeling wounded and trying to find someone to blame for your pain and suffering. Difficulty forgiving.

Melanoma

Feeling vulnerable and unprotected. Making limiting choices that don't work and then stubbornly sticking with them. Internal aggression that bursts to the surface. Feeling unsatisfied with life. Thinking is this all there is? Resistance to growing, changing and expanding. Lack of trust in yourself. Refusing to look deeper. Wanting to be told what to do, how to think and how to live.

Cancer

Feeling limited, angry, fearful, out of control. Carrying wounds from the past. Not feeling good enough, shrinking inside and attacking yourself from within. Feeling like guilt, grief and uncertainty are eating away at your body.

Tumours

Shock, fear, trauma. Suppressing emotional hurt. Feelings of anger, revenge and resentment. Difficulty in believing and trusting others, feeling unlovable. Believing that nobody cares about you.

Widowedwithkids.co.uk

Patience

I used to be a very impatient person and would want something straightaway. It has taken me a long time to be fully patient with my life. I was always so busy and focused on the destination rather than embracing the journey. Now I focus on the present moment and know that what will be will be.

I do believe now that you should stop suffering with impatience and start being happy and fully patient.

Shifting into patience brings peace and freedom.

Strip away the drama and show up as who you really are. I lived in my drama for far too long.

Get out of the shade, the sun is shining for all of us. We just have to take the step to get out of the shade and allow ourselves to shine. It often feels scary to take that step, but when you do, it is so worth it.

New Relationship With Myself

This is what I've learnt.

I do believe it's important to build a relationship with yourself before you get into a new relationship. To love yourself unconditionally before you can love anyone else.

Joy is within you, not outside you.

I was looking for the joy in a new relationship and I do believe that is why both my relationships broke down.

All I have is inside me, it was just a matter of finding it.

Love is joy and happiness within.

Stay true to who you are.

Don't compare yourself to others.

'Nobody's life is perfect and if you enjoy what you have, life can be perfect for you'.....Viktor Frankl

Grief is a horrible, painful journey and it can take years to move forward. Each person's journey is unique to them.

Many people kiss photos or talk to photos of their loved ones.

The pain never goes, it simply becomes less intense over time.

Widowedwithkids.co.uk

The Other Side Of Me

I am now aware of my passion in life and I can now say 'what for?', rather than 'why me?'.

I'm going to sound a bit woo-woo now.

I had not really used essential oils before until I met a lady who was a dōTERRA consultant. dōTERRA sells natural essential oils. I began asking her lots of questions, and we met up. She said that she would like to try the emotional oils on me first.

She got me to smell the emotional oils and she said the one that I didn't like was the one that I needed. The names were all covered and most of them I liked, until I smelt one that really made my stomach turn. I pushed it away and said that was disgusting.

She said that was the one that I needed, and my ego was saying, 'I am not spending my money on that, it is horrible.'

She gave me a sample to try and told me to use it when I went to bed. When I woke up the next morning, I jumped out of bed and felt fantastic. I used it that day too as I was at a meeting all day, and I had a great day.

I spoke to her in the evening and found out the essential oil was 'Passion'.

Since I have used that oil, I have found my passion in life.

I do believe my purpose in life is to help and support people like you who are grieving, grieving so deeply that you don't know what to do. You feel so lonely, how will you survive without your loved one?

I now value my self-worth as I have been through this traumatic process, and I love myself unconditionally, and I trust myself and go with what feels right in my heart.

I have found my purpose in life and my passion. And that is to support you.

Being me

People will love me just being me.
Which wasn't something I'd been able to see.
Now there's nobody else I'd rather be.
Life's such a gift by just being me.

By Steve Buxton

My Journey Through The Eyes Of My Friends

My beautiful friends have written me some letters to say how much I have grown and developed over the years, and become the Rose in Bloom.

Her sensible advice. When I met Sharon at the turn of the century she was a different person.

Far removed from the confident, successful and eloquent woman she's since blossomed into, the girl I knew was quiet, shy and without a shred of the self-assurance she now possesses.

Sharon and I met in the school playground: me, stressed and rushing to collect my sons after a busy day at work; she, chatting to other mums with her son Oliver asleep in his buggy.

I needed help with the logistics of juggling a family and business, whilst Sharon needed time away from school to focus on Oliver. We met, we chatted, we liked each other instantly, and so our friendship began. We helped each other with a rota for taking and picking up the children from school. Many mothers do this, but our situation developed into a closeness and trust that goes beyond merely waving our respective kids along the path.

By the time Simon became critically ill I had watched my friend remain seemingly cheerful and 'together' as she nursed him over the course of several months. And when this kind, lovely man passed away, her strength amazed everyone.

Where many women in Sharon's shoes would have fallen apart, she defiantly gathered herself up and determined to make the best life possible for her children. From her initial studies in herbalism and her voluntary work as a bereavement counsellor, she has accomplished an unimaginable, incredible amount in the past few years.

Qualifying as a fully-fledged counsellor and hypnotherapist with a thriving practice has been such an impressive feat, and publishing her story is the icing on the cake. Sharon is warm, generous and caring; I'm certain that the hard work and passion she injects into every project will ensure that this book is a success. And her compassion will surely help bereaved parents immensely.

Renée Wallen

****

Widowedwithkids.co.uk

When I met Sharon back in approx. 1999/2000, she was a warm, friendly lady. We met because our children had made friends at nursery school. We didn't pick each other out as such, and I certainly don't remember Sharon being a strong noticeable character amongst the Mums....our girls loved their playdates together and we both clicked.

I remember Sharon being welcoming and very into her children. We didn't have similar hobbies but I soon got to know her well and we both had a laugh together and came to support each other as Sharon's husband took a new job and a move away from the area was being planned. I was used to my husband being away and we discussed the adjustments necessary to manage it.

Sharon then spoke to me about her concerns with her baby/toddler's development and I encouraged her to pursue further support in understanding his needs. She was not an over emotional person by any means and quite accepting and matter of fact......and appeared to remain calm and patient on the surface in these stressful times, as she waited patiently for her husband to find their next "right" home and settle into his new all-encompassing job away from home and began to understand that things were not right with her son and this would need to be sorted when they moved. Sharon also then acknowledged with me Simon's health challenge as a secondary cancer arrived in his tongue....and a probable unknown journey was unfolding there....

I didn't sense that Sharon had a wide circle of friends...she and her hubby were quite self-sufficient in their own family. They were very warm and we kept in touch when they moved away. Distance was a challenge and I tried to keep in touch with visits when possible....but this dissipated and unfortunately I was not able to visit much during Simon's illness and during the early years of Oliver's diagnosis.

However, I knew Sharon had a lot to cope with and I admired her always for her bravery. She was not one to ask for help or show desperation.

Eventually we got back in touch and Sharon managed to come down to stay when Simon had died. I realised then her fear of driving but she trusted Sat Nav and got to me. It was a nightmare her getting home as Sat Nav didn't work and the journey was terrible.....I realised how much she had had to go out of her comfort zone just to drive, let alone bringing her Autistic son to a new environment for two nights. She was a brave lady!

Things then went "quiet" with Sharon...she was coping with her challenges and I had family problems arising and couldn't give the extra time and attention as I had before, but I kept in touch when I could. I realised the hole left in Sharon's life without Simon as he was the pillar of the family I think at that point.

However, Sharon kept working on her life ahead and had strength to tackle the challenges of finding the right support for her son and keeping her daughter's life as smooth as possible with limited family support. I always found her matter of fact and therefore not a complaining person......but I wondered if she had become emotionally shut down at some level.

When we started to reconnect again I could see Sharon's want to chat more and her ability to explore the world in a different way and see there were different things she would need to encounter without Simon, for the sake of her children and then herself. .....she always had great interest in my news and we spoke about my Homeopathy training.....we could talk more straight to each other and I had such admiration for a lady who was clearly stuck on some levels with all that she had been through, but was desperately trying to emerge.....and lo and behold, Sharon was emerging! What an inspiration! I too was stuck on some levels and Sharon was able to listen and offer me support too.

More recently, Sharon has emerged further and I am learning so much from her! She is a brave and fun lady who still likes to stay in her comfort zone on some levels, yet knows the benefits, and loves going out of it regularly and bravely to move forward in life that she has come to realise can be so much more enjoyable, even against the odds. She has compassion for others and took it into bereavement counselling, and then furthered her personal development with hypnosis and life coaching....and then entered the world of natural health with the start of her homeopathy training. She is so wonderful at helping people but in a very subtle way.......She is much more carefree and keeps positivity high on her daily attitude to life, whilst also being able to be down to earth...wonderful gifts, and I am lucky to have her as a friend. She can stay in her lane well!

Sharon is more able to be in the spot light now and can hold her own in public situations to a far higher level! Her inquisitive mind is active now and I think she is living life to a far fuller degree than a few years ago! If Simon was alive, I do not know if she would be as strong in her own abilities......she may have stayed in his shadow as it would have been comfortable and easy.....I don't actually know...but whatever, he will be proud of her now and Sharon certainly shows pride and pleasure in her own achievements, herself, on the journey she has in recent years in particularly, grabbed fully by the horns and ridden in self-growth and fulfilment....which has taken a lot of work and perhaps we haven't always appreciated just how much work!

Love you Sharon! What a gift of a friend you are to me! Soul sisters!

Ali Lomax

****

A strong but beautiful woman was what I saw at our first meeting alongside the beautiful bride that stood so graciously in the framed wedding photo along for everyone to see.

In later years she showed great courage and defiance as together they fought the cancer that Simon endured.

The days, months after the passing of our dear Simon, Sharon quite understandably became a shell of her previous self. Gone was the vibrancy and wit that I had so often experienced in our relationship and it was with a gentle manner I witnessed friends and family tread carefully around her.

With time it was Sharon's courage that once again shone through, encapsulating her to become what I see now is a woman with confidence, self-belief, knowing that she can conquer her fears and live life to its fullest.

Aruna Mandal Lodhia

****

Ever since I've known you, you have always been a very strong character. You just get on with whatever is thrown at you. You were a devoted wife to Simon and are a wonderful mother to Sophie and Oliver. You helped Oliver by giving him the best chances in life and the way you were with your children is shown by what amazing adults they have become.

During Simon's illness you stayed positive and keeping 'normality' for Sophie and Oliver as much as possible. You went through every step of his illness with him only thinking of others and not yourself. We were very close friends at this time and I was pregnant with my third child. When Simon passed away you were devastated although he was no longer suffering. Again you made sure everyone around you were coping. I made sure you were ok. You really are a selfless person who thinks of others before yourself and deserve the success you have today.

Naomi Davis

****

When I first met Sharon, I remember feeling like she was living under a dark cloud and was somewhat negative and as the years have gone on she has become a confident, outgoing, strong woman and a wonderful friend and confidant and has always been there for me to listen and coach. I'm so proud of the woman she has become.

Justine Conway

****

Sharon is my longest standing friend of now 46 years. We became friends at Junior School when we were (11?). I have fond memories of that time, birthday parties, Yorkshire terrier, youth club and Hampstead, where we went often as young adults. We even took our first holiday together, alone, to Italy at the age of (17?). I worked in a corporate world and Sharon was a budding beautician for Lancôme – I remember because she used to give me lots of samples!

Whilst our adult lives since then took very different paths and for most of it, even to date, we have travelled our separate roads, we have always remained connected somewhere in our souls throughout our lives and never lost touch.

Sharon has had a lot to navigate in her life and I am so proud of the incredible woman she has blossomed into – helping not just others, but by also becoming the best version of herself in the process.

She truly is a Rose that has Bloomed, from Lancôme counter-girl to a soon to be author! Sharon, my special friend, I commend you!

Jo

****

I admire you. You are always smiling.

You are a fantastic mother.

You are brave – You have faced your fears, you have brought up your children on your own,

You have come through serious illnesses; you have not given up.

You are courageous – you face your fears and talk about them to others to inspire them.

You are approachable – (who ever feels they can't say hello to you and talk to you needs to have a word with me (Mags)

You are fun loving and enjoy life in a lively, loving, light-hearted way, and are spirited.

You are Adventurous – when you want something you go out and do it and don't let anyone get in your way.

You are Humble – your achievements are amazing (I don't think you know quite how amazing)

You are Formidable – you are a definite person to look up to, you have admiration, awe and are inspiring.

You are Impressive – how you deal with things, different hurdles good and bad and how you believe different avenues of life.

You are Beautiful – inside and out.

You have a warm smile and eyes.

You are Generous – in spirit, always willing to listen, give advice and spend time with people.

You are Sincere (which I love about you).You are open (which I love about you)

You are genuine (which I love about you)

You are ambitious – you are excited about writing a book

You are easy going – you are so easy to talk to and get along with, and always looking to help.

You are Persistent – you don't give up and are always on the ball

You are Trusting – you listen to others, and you trust their advice and give recommendations a go.

You are Amiable – you are kind, warm and friendly to everybody.

You are Kind – you always know when to say the right thing to cheer someone up.

You are Considerate – you always show concern for others and look out for them too......that's why I became friends with you.

You go and get what you want, and if you have a goal or vision in mind that motivates and drives you, you do it.

You are Unassuming – you are an awesome lady but you don't go around bragging about it, in fact I don't think you even know that you are so awesome.

You are Resourceful – you have the creativity and the things around you to tackle a problem.

You see solutions, sometimes obvious ones that others don't see.

You are Exuberant – you are full of joy and have a lot of energy to show, you are always happy and the energy oozes out of you when you speak about a lot of things....especially your book.

You are Affectionate – you always have warmth and fondness for Me and Steve and for my loved ones. It shines through.

Love Margarita Genovesa

****

My Morning Rituals

I always used to snooze my alarm clock and I used to set my alarm an hour earlier than I needed to get up. This was something I had done since I was a teenager, and it became a habit. Thinking about that now, it seems so crazy.

Anna Garcia, my coach, told me to move my clock to the other side of my bed so I would have to get out of bed to turn it off. It was really hard in the beginning, but I know now how much better it is for me.

After doing Anna's mastery programme, I started getting up at 6am every day and, since Covid-19, I have been getting up at 5am so that I have some quality 'me time' before Oliver gets up.

Before I gave up the sugar, I had extraordinarily little energy and would often nap during the day, but since coming off the sugar, I very rarely nap during the day now.

Here is my morning routine:

1. I do not snooze my alarm.

2. I stand up, do some yoga and stretching.

3. I meditate, listen to my thoughts, and observe them, and say thank you for any thought I do not want and do not want to get stuck with it. An excellent app that I use is called 'Headspace'.

4. I do not look at my phone for at least an hour after waking.

5. I get my clothes ready the night before for the following morning.

6. I smile for no reason and take three deep breaths.

7. I forgive myself for yesterday's mistakes.

8. I say what I am grateful for.

9. I acknowledge myself for what I have done well.

10. I set my intentions for the day, who am I going to be, for example, peaceful, confident and happy.

11. I hold a vision of what I want, then I imagine it, feel it, and give thanks for it. I might imagine how I will feel when I have released my extra weight, for example, free and light, and I then tap into those feelings.

12. I decide how am I going to love myself today, for example, by exercising, eating well, being kind, sleeping well, being patient, relaxing, telling myself I am enough, and looking in the mirror and telling myself that I love me.
13. In my journal, I write down all that I appreciate in life, which goes deeper than gratitude.

It was not easy to do all these things in the beginning and there are odd days when I do not always do it, but I try my hardest to make this my morning ritual. I do feel I have a better day if I do these things at the start of my day.

Meditation

Meditation is excellent for training your mind and to redirect your thoughts, rather than getting stuck in them.

Meditation has helped me to understand that I am part of the human experience, and that we are all unique and we all experience pain, loss, fear and joy. I have come to realise that my fear and pain are no longer consuming me now. When the intensity of the pain hits me, I have learnt to return to deep breathing so that I can then ground myself.

By doing this, I am a better person, less anxious and less controlling. And even when life gets very challenging, I feel calmer day by day.

I meditate every day and concentrate on my breathing for just ten to twenty minutes a day. It gives me time to be me, and then I can stand out for my children and everyone around me. I can engage in my life in a full and rich manner.

It is okay to feel different emotions as they are a part of us, fear, sadness, anger, guilt, and to be present for them all and let them pass.

We all have on average 60,000 thoughts a day. When meditation was first introduced to me, I had no idea what to do, and I just used to say to myself, 'I can't do this'.

Can you imagine your mind as the blue sky and your thoughts are like the clouds that just come and go. Sometimes the clouds are very dark and heavy, but in meditation, you learn to let your thoughts go.

If meditation is new to you, start with just five to ten minutes a day to give your busy mind a rest. Then gradually increase the amount of time you meditate.

It took me about six months to fully master how to do it and now I love doing it, and it has become part of my morning ritual.

I found it difficult to meditate on my own in the beginning and I prefer a guided meditation.

Affirmations

"I let go of fear. I let go of pain. I live in love."

Whatever you think you become.

Affirmations for me help to change your beliefs, they help to change your mind-set.

For example, I had a brain tumour in 1986. I have always said I have a poor short-term memory and I could never remember anything unless I wrote it down.

Since I have been saying every day, 'my memory is improving every day', my memory has really improved so much.

You really can change your programming to overcome and change your beliefs.

Feel each affirmation as you say it, write it down and say it every day.

Here are some examples of the affirmations I say daily. Some are from Laura Helen, my publisher, some are from the Jon Gabriel Method and some are from Deepak Chopra.

Love
- I love who I have become
- I love all of me
- I am worthy of love
- Today I remember to love everything and everyone I come in contact with

Self-worth
- I am strong
- I am enough
- I am confident in new situations
- I forgive me
- I have everything I need inside of me
- I am confident
- I am an incredible mum
- I am here to make a positive impact
- Like the morning sun, I will rise and continue to shine
- I am free of judgement
- I have a good memory
- I am going to smile every day

Forgiveness

- I forgive me
- I forgive me for anything I may have said in the past
- I acknowledge my faults and forgive myself completely
- When I make a mistake, I stop brooding over it, I learn from it and move on
- I am aware of my faults and forgive myself
- I am willing to forgive myself and set myself free

Health

- I radiate health and vitality, I naturally release excess weight
- I nourish my body, I effortlessly absorb nutrients
- I have digestive power, I digest effortlessly and easily
- I eat life force foods, I am vitality
- I radiate love, I love my body
- I radiate healing light, I am life force vitality
- I radiate health and vitality, I naturally release excess weight
- I am effortlessly fit, I am my ideal body
- I am protected, it is safe to let go of the excess weight
- I am safe, safe to release the excess weight
- I am strong, secure and grounded, I easily release the excess weight
- I have power, power to create my ideal body, ideal life, I let go of excess weight
- I forgive, I love, I accept, I forgive, love, accept my body, my life

- I am free, free to let go of excess weight
- I am at peace, I peacefully release excess weight
- I am calm, I calmly release excess weight
- I am guided, guided to my ideal body, ideal life
- I allow success, success in weight loss, success in life
- I am worthy, I am deserving, deserving of my ideal body, ideal life
- I trust, I am guided, guided to my ideal body, ideal life

Abundance

- I allow abundance into my life, abundance effortlessly flows to me
- I hold all the abundance that surrounds me
- Today I focus on what I want to attract in my life
- I invite unlimited abundance into my life
- Today I embrace my potential to be, do and have whatever I dream
- Everything I deserve is within me
- I use my conscious intention to manifest my dreams
- Through the law of pure potentiality, I can create anything, anywhere, anytime
- Today and every day, I give what I want to receive
- Today I make great choices because they are made with full awareness
- I expect and accept abundance to flow easily to me
- My actions and desires are supported by cosmic intelligence
- As I let go of the need to arrange my life, the universe brings abundant good to me

- Money will return to me tenfold
- Every moment of everyday I live my life abundantly
- I am going to travel first-class on an aeroplane
- Today I treat myself to moments of luxury
- As I live in present awareness, I live the magic of synchro destiny

Gratitude

- Today I remember to be grateful
- I move through my days light-hearted and carefree knowing all is well
- I celebrate my unity with all life knowing we are all one
- I am grateful for so much in my life

Hope and trust

- The power of hope is here every day
- Hope is my source of strength
- Hope makes me strong and secure
- In hope I am fearless
- I feel the fear and do it anyway
- There is a way I can fulfil my true purpose in life
- I have every hope in the world
- I trust in core self at every moment
- I find a reason to hope in every situation
- Today I activate my hope
- I trust in life because I trust myself
- I will never give up

113

Mantras

A mantra is a group of words, sounds or phrases which is used as a tool to help calm the nervous system and the mind when recited. When you give your mind something to focus on, you can slow your thoughts down. Here are some mantras you can repeat if you are feeling overwhelmed or anxious:

1.   I am strong, supported and abundant.

2.   I am the creator of my entire reality.

3.   I am worthy of pursuing my passion and purpose.

4.   I am love, I give love, I am open to love.

5.   I am in alignment with my truth.

6.   I am in connection with my spirit and I trust my intuition.

Meaningful Poems

Me: Hello

God: Hello

Me: I'm falling apart. Can you put me back together?

God: I'd rather not.

Me: Why?

God: Because you're not a puzzle.

Me: What about all the pieces of my life that fall to the ground?

God: Leave them there for a while and then decide if you need to take any of those pieces back.

Me: You don't understand! I'm breaking!

God: No, you don't understand. You're transcending, evolving.

What you feel are growing pains. You're getting rid of the things and people in your life that are holding you back. The pieces are not falling down. The pieces are being put in place. Relax. Take a deep breath and let those things you no longer need fall down. Stop clinging to pieces that are no longer for you. Let them fall. Let them go.

Me: Once I start doing that, what will I have left?

God: Only the best pieces of yourself.

Me: I'm afraid to change.

God: I keep telling you: YOU'RE NOT CHANGING! YOU'RE BECOMING!

Me: Becoming, who?

God: Becoming who I created you to be! A person of light, love, charity, hope, courage, joy, mercy, grace and compassion. I made you for so much more than those shallow pieces you decided to adorn yourself with and that you cling to with so much greed and fear. Let those things fall off you. I love you! Don't change! Become! Don't change! Become! Become who I want you to be, who I created. I'm going to keep telling you this until you remember.

ME: There goes another piece.

God: Yes. Let it be like this.

Me: So, I am not broken

God: No, but you're breaking the darkness, like dawn. It's a new day. Become! Become who you really are!

From my friend Rupi

The next three poems are written by Christian Bare, who is 27 years old and a widower. His wife Ashley was tragically taken when her and her mother Rosie were hit by a wrong-way driver. Just two miles from their home. She was pregnant with their first child and five days before the accident they found out they were having a little boy. The doctors didn't know if Rosie was going to make it, but fortunately she has recovered.

****

What They See Vs What They Don't

They see my smile, not my cries.

They see my laugh, not my brokenness inside.

They see me going on day by day, not my pain that could never go away.

They see me moving forward one step at a time, they don't see how half of my heart is missing on the inside.

As they see me move forward, take steps, even start to date, they don't see me crying alone, hating, thinking about the thought of moving forward and going on without you.

They see me smile, say "I'm okay, I'm hanging in there".

They don't see the hours of looking at pictures, and videos, thinking of what was, and what was supposed to be that no longer is.

It's okay that you see what you see, but when you left far too early how could I ever still be me.

See when you left so did I, my better half is in heaven, I can't ever say goodbye. 💔 .

Love you always and forever, missing you today more than yesterday.

In loving memory of Ashley Bare and Christian Douglas
Bare Jr

****

Remember me

Remember me,
Remember me, when you're home
Remember me, when you're alone
Remember me, when you smile
Remember me, when you cry
Remember me, when you move forward and don't ask why
Remember me, and you'll never have to say goodbye.
For I will always be with you in your heart,
Remember me always and we'll never be apart.
Remember me when you achieve.
Remember me, and know that you will still succeed.
Remember me, and always believe
That I am with you always far and near, if you need me I'm always here.
I am that feeling on your cheek when you shed a tear.
Remember me, and continue to be that amazing person that I fell in love with.
Remember me, and know that you have so much left to give.
Remember me, and I'll always live.
Remember you always I will.
Until we meet again, love you always and forever.
Missing you today more than yesterday

In loving memory of Ashley Bare and Christian Douglas Bare Jr

One Step Forward, No Step Gained

One step forward, No step gained
I take one step forward, but still feel the same pain
One step forward, No step gained
As I take one step forward, half of my heart remains, at square one that could never change.
When you left so did I, I know this to be true
Because when I said I do we become one, no longer two
How can I move one step forward when I gave my all to you.
One step forward, no step gained.
This grief is so exhausting, I feel so drained.
As I move one step forward, my love for you remains stronger than ever.
As I move one step forward, I carry you in my heart where you'll never depart.

Ashley Bare and Christian Douglas Bare Jr

****

Being me

People will love me just being me.
Which wasn't something I'd been able to see.
Now there's nobody else I'd rather be.
Life's such a gift by just being me.

By Steve Buxton

Goodbye Sorry Monkey

I stand tall and proud
Proud to face fear in the face
To stair right back at you
I see you; yes you
My sorry monkey on my back
Monkey holding me back; shackled in my pain
Pain that led to my suffering
Sorry monkey with all your chatter
Sorry monkey on my back
Sorry you see me
Sorry for being here
Sorry for breathing
Sorry for being me
Sorry monkey; I am done with you
You hear me
Yes you
I no longer need you
You are no longer welcome here
Your residence is over
I no longer need your permission
Or seek your approval
To be me
My suffering is no more
I am free
Free from your sorry shackles
Free from the doubt, the fear and sorry mocking
Free to unapologetically be me

Free to love
Love now reigns
Love is my light
Love is more beautiful than you ever were
Sorry monkey; be on your way now

Farewell sorry monkey; monkey no more on my back

By Pippa Mackenzie-Smith

From my Beautiful friend Pippa Mackenzie-Smith who I met at Relationship Intensive by Anna Garcia, and to whom I was always saying sorry for being me.

****

Quotes That Mean Something To Me

"You get in life what you have the courage to ask for."

"Happiness is ready made and it comes from your own actions."

"You can't fall if you don't climb, there's no point living your whole life on the ground."

"Strive not to be a success, but rather to be of value."

"Life is a marathon not a sprint, take your time, there is no rush or force."

"Difficult roads often lead to beautiful destinations."

"We are all different flowers from the same garden."

"Happiness is an inside job; you will never be truly happy with anyone until you are happy with yourself."

"You can't start the next chapter if you keep re-reading the last chapter."

"Don't be discouraged, it's often the last key on the bunch that opens the lock."

"Nobody's life is perfect, but if you enjoy what you have life can be perfect for you."

"Nobody truly dies until they are forgotten."

"From acorns oak trees grow.....Take baby steps and watch your growth."

"Fear does not cause death, it prevents life"

One Of My Coaches – Anna Garcia

Anna Garcia is an international best-selling author and one of the UK's foremost experts on relationships. She is a playful, vivacious and inspirational facilitator/relationship specialist committed to guiding individuals through their journey of self-discovery back to love and peace after painful relationships and events.

She is the founder of Relationships Intensive, the UK's No.1 relationship seminar for women. This programme has changed the lives of thousands of women since 2016.

Anna has dedicated the past ten years to working with women to help them discover how extraordinary they are, to have them know their power and to understand how to be in their relationships with others and, most importantly, with themselves after a loss or relationship break-up. She has been showing women how to reconnect with their own journey again, whether they are in a marriage, or are single or separated. She has been gifting this to women throughout the world

About the Author

Sharon thought she had the perfect life, she was married to a wonderful man and had two beautiful children. A little girl and a little a boy. In her eyes, it couldn't have been any better. Although in other people's, eyes it probably wasn't perfect as her husband was in remission from pancreatic cancer, and her son had complex special needs and was very challenging.

Nine years later on New Year's Eve, Simon's cancer had come back. Not exactly the new year they had hoped for!

That is when Sharon's world came crashing down, Simon had all the usual cancer treatment and was very sick, and after 6 months Simon finally lost his life.

Sharon also felt like she had lost her life too, she lost her husband, her soul mate, her best friend, her children's father. She just didn't want to be here anymore and thank God she had to for her children.

Sharon only got out of bed in the morning to get her children ready for school, and felt so lonely, lost and overwhelmed.

Many years later and after being in two serious relationships, Sharon realised that the only relationship that was missing in her life was a relationship with herself. Sharon never loved herself.

And after doing a lot of personal development Sharon has now found her true passion in life, and for the last 14 years

Sharon has been supporting families going through the grieving process. She has found what her soul is here for, and that is to share with you what has taken her 17 years to discover. To help you come out of the darkest and most painful place, and to help you see the light again.

Sharon believes her darkest times have been a gift to share with others.

Author's Resources

I have included the resources, such as books, films, coaches, and therapies that helped me get through my darkest times, in the hope that they will help you too on your journey.

Therapists

Ali Lomax is the one who first introduced me to homoeopathy therapies and helped me transition to the natural help that is available.

June Lawrence is an incredible lady who helps you raise your vibration, heal yourself and get what you really want.

Laura Helen is my amazing life & business coach who really helped me face my fears and find myself again, helping me find my mission to serve and help you, she is also my book publisher.

Gozi Halina is an energy healer, coach and a Theta healer, who taught me how to listen to my body.

Chris Hill helped me beat my sugar addiction.

Rodney Pedroza is a portrait photographer who helps you find yourself through the experience.

Anna Garcia is a relationship and life coach who taught me how to have a relationship with myself. You can read more about her in 'One of my coaches – Anna Garcia'.

Books

'The Secret Language of Your Body', by Inna Segal

Websites

Gozi Halina – www.gozphilosophy.com

Anna Garcia – www.relationshipsintensive.com

Chris Hill – www.beatmyaddiction.com

Rodney Pedroza – www.rodneypedroza.com

Posture – www.symmetryofmotion.com

Ali Lomax – www.horsleyhomeopathy.co.uk

June Lawrence – www.jl-lifebydesign.com

Laura Helen – www.booksboostbusiness.co.uk

Children's resources

'Muddles, Puddles and Sunshine', by Diana Crossley

'The Secret C: Straight Talking about Cancer', by Julie A. Stokes

Disney 'Inside Out' film

Winston's Wish – an excellent charity for child bereavement support – www.winstonswish.o

Learn how to take care of yourself while guiding your kids through their grief.

Nothing prepares you for parenting after your partner dies.

FREE 3-Part Video Series Of Help and Support
Get instant access!

www.widowedwithkids.co.uk

Homeopathy with Ali Lomax

A Homeopathic appointment is quite different to a typical appointment with a doctor; it gives the practitioner time to really get to know the individual and understand how things are playing out for them in all aspects of their life....this is known as a Holistic approach.

The remedies I then prescribe match each individual's symptoms and energy which allow them to process their grief thoroughly and in a manageable way. Emotions are therefore well supported not suppressed and this is key when working with grief. We understand the way emotional and physical symptoms so often need combining.

What is so great is that Homeopathic remedies are very gentle on the system with no side effects, toxicity or addictive qualities.

Homeopathy works with babies, children and adults ...... it is a wonderful method of support in nearly all health complaints and therefore ideal for use on our general health and wellbeing in everyday life, a little bit like having a first aid kit at the ready!

Please do feel free to get in touch to find out more: **www.horsleyhomeopathy.co.uk.**

I see patients in clinic or via video setting if more practical and for appointments made outside of the U.K.

https://horsleyhomeopathy.co.uk/

JUNE LAWERENCE
Life by Design

I have especially designed a course so you can learn the art of unconditional love, acceptance, and healing.

During this course you learn how to feel safe again, improve your relationship with sleep & face your memories with courage and compassion.

Together we discover how to get out of your head, and into your heart.

Allowing yourself to be transported to beautiful and exotic locations with my guided meditations.

We learn how to fall in love with ourselves, and how to feel whole again.

Use the QR code or the link below to connect & receive a half-hour free consultation.

https://www.jl-lifebydesign.com
Tel +447793004812

Has someone told you:

-You should really write a book about that!

But you have no idea how to start
writing your book?

Maybe you have considered writing a book to share
your journey for some time now?

Maybe you've got an idea for a book but don't
know how to get it on paper?

Maybe you don't think of yourself as an author or writer?
And having that hindering your
production in writing a book?

Or maybe it could be that you already have a brilliant idea
but don't know the process to get a book published?

— — — — — — —

*"I am here to tell you —
your idea is brilliant! By sharing your
story in a book, you will help your
readers overcome and get through
their own challenges."*

— — — — — — —

Learn how to start to write a book:
Join Our FREE 3-day Video Series
That Shows You Exactly How To Do It.
www.booksboostbusiness.com/3-video-series

Made in the USA
Las Vegas, NV
18 January 2021

16125956R00085